Tactical Entrepreneur

The Entrepreneur's Game Plan

Second Edition

By Brian J. Hazelgren

This publication is intended to provide accurate and authoritative information
in regard to the subject matter covered. It is sold with the understanding
that the publisher is not engaged in rendering legal, accounting, or
other professional service. If legal advise or other expert assistance is
required, the services of a competent professional should be sought.

ISBN-13:   978-0-9772025-1-5
ISBN-10:   0-9772025-1-8

Published by: Sortis Publishing
Mesa, Arizona
www.sortispublishing.com

Table of Contents

Opening Statement

Congratulations! The fact that you are reading this book tells me you are about to embark on an exciting journey, discovering the challenges and rewards of being an entrepreneur and of managing or starting your own small business. And, because you are reading this, I know another thing—you are smart enough to realize that owning your own business does not mean going it completely alone. You have made a wise choice. You will find that *Tactical Entrepreneur: The Entrepreneur's Game Plan* contains a wealth of extremely important and valuable information—information that can help you navigate the often treacherous process of business ownership.

Owning a business, or *entrepreneurship,* is all about having the freedom of doing things your way, but that is only possible as you take calculated risks in working toward an obtainable goal. In this manual, I am going to teach you not only how to start a small business, but how to learn from others who have already made the mistakes for you—and how to take that knowledge and mold it into a success story of your own.

I am literally going to hand you an immensely expensive education in business, all for the price of what you paid for this book. This education will not only save you thousands, if not hundreds of thousands, of dollars in lessons learned, this book will also show you how to establish a business that will help you make a great deal of money over and above those savings. After all, the freedom to do what you want in growing your own business is one thing, but how much freedom do you actually have if you can't pay the bills, and have a little left over for yourself? The principles in this book, if followed, will allow you to have a lot left over for you and your family, or for whatever you want to do with it.

If I sound a little braggadocios, I don't mean to. The fact is, I have obtained an expensive education of what works and what doesn't in the world of business. I have made a lot of money running businesses, and I have lost a lot of money based on foolish choices I have made. Although I do have a college degree, I also have earned a PhD several times over from UHK.

As you may already know, UHK stands for the *University of Hard Knocks*. I have what you would refer to as "street smarts," which I gained from more than two decades of going after my dreams and not sitting back waiting for things to come to me. I love to share what I have learned with others. This is one thing that always resonates to the top for me. That is why I teach Entrepreneurship at one of the top-rated universities in the United States. I have a passion for learning, teaching and succeeding. I am very good at what I do because I love to learn and I enjoy seeing others succeed based on a few principles that they might have learned from me.

In four previous books—*Secrets to Writing Powerful Business Plans, Your First Business Plan, The Complete Book of Business Plans,* and *The Business Game Plan*—I introduced valuable resources for writing powerful and persuasive business plans. In *Tactical Entrepreneur,* I expand on those concepts, applying my experiences from many years of teaching Entrepreneurship at the University of Utah and from my business successes and "learning experiences."

The purpose of this book is to assist you in your entrepreneurial ventures; my ultimate goal is to help you find success in owning and operating a small business, or even running a department within a large organization. The journey of entrepreneurship is incredibly challenging, yet highly enjoyable… one that will open up an entire new world. That world is known to millions as the "road to success…the one less traveled," even, "the road to financial freedom." I would like to help you get on that road, point you in the direction of the success you are seeking and see you reach your goal of thriving in business and of accomplishing something truly worthwhile.

Take these principles, and apply them to the business of your dreams, Whether you are just starting out, or whether you already have an ongoing enterprise, I guarantee you will learn something new that will turn a light on for you with a new idea; a newly found enthusiasm for what you are doing; even a sincere justification that what you are doing makes sense and is perfect for you.

Owning and operating a small business is obviously a big step, but if you carefully plan each step of the journey (as best you can) and then execute the plan, you will be very happy and satisfied with your business endeavors. Vincent Van Gogh said: "Great things are not done by impulse, but by a series of small things brought together." This book is meant to provide you with some of those small things that will yield greatness for you and your business.

Indeed, *Tactical Entrepreneur* is the game plan for greatness. Thanks for your confidence and for allowing me, through this book, to serve as your coach and mentor. For now, sit back and enjoy the incredible experience of learning more about your successful future! Every minute you spend reading and learning from this book will be highly valuable to your journey to the top. This is positively a journey worth taking.

Very Sincerely and Many Thanks,

Brian Hazelgren

CHAPTER ONE:
Entrepreneurship Training Camp

Start Your Business

Starting a business and being an entrepreneur. What an exciting time, and what a busy time! You have decided to take on what will probably be the most challenging thing you have ever done in your life. Yes, it can be very rewarding and fulfilling. Yet, make no mistake about it; it will demand every one of your resources and will stretch every bit of your skills and talents. An entrepreneur is defined as...*one who organizes, manages, and assumes the risks of a business or enterprise.*

In the entrepreneurship courses I teach at the University of Utah, I start off the semester with phrases like: "How many of you want to become an *entre-manure*? How much have you researched about *entre-manureship*? How many of you are already an *entre-manure*?"

This gets the students' attention, and it is rather comical to watch the looks on their faces. Inevitably, several students will turn to their neighbors and whisper, "Is he saying that right? It sounds like he is saying 'manure.' Who is this bozo anyway?"

We all get a good laugh out of it when I confess that owning a business is often like running a manure factory; it's usually piled high and deep, and you are wading in the middle of "it" most of the time.

I don't want to scare you. I only want to set a basic foundation. My job is to teach you the good, the bad, and the ugly about entrepreneurship. From reading this guide, you will learn firsthand what it takes to succeed in business and how to stay away from the pitfalls. This doesn't mean that you will not stumble along the way, but I can at least give you some of the background and the foundation to build on.

I want you to know that, aside from all the hype and excitement, owning your own business requires good planning, hard work, strategy, capital resources, sales, good people, sound management practices, good suppliers, a good product or service, technology, brand identity, enough insurance, contacts, and about a thousand other things I could list here…if you want to succeed.

This first chapter presents some of the basics to think about as you plan for business ownership. Then, in the remaining chapters, you will find several tools, worksheets and explanations that will help you determine the steps required to start your business as well as things you need to know to keep it afloat. You will learn:

- What it means to own your own business
- How to determine the right business for you, plus the pros and cons of buying a business
- How to evaluate your chances for success

Plus, in this guide, you'll be shown:

- What a business plan can do for you
- How to gather the information needed to formulate a business plan
- How to write, organize and present your plan, as well as what documents to include and why

With the information presented in *Tactical Entrepreneur*, you also will be able to conduct an analysis of your market to locate customers and understand their buying patterns. You will be able to identify your Unique Selling Advantage (USA) and will have the direction you need to formulate a marketing strategy and a sales strategy. You also will have ideas for taking care of the customers you attract, to ensure that they will buy from you in the future.

Responsibilities of Ownership

It's estimated that in the United States, only about 30 percent of all startups are still in business after five years. In some states, the number is only about 10 percent. These are startling numbers; and, yet, they are somewhat understandable. Most small business owners are too busy to plan for the future, or at least they think they are too busy. The fact is, the better you understand the challenges ahead of you and the better you prepare yourself for those challenges, the more likely it is that you'll be one of the survivors.

Probably the two most common reasons that a business doesn't succeed come down to (1) poor management because the owner lacks the necessary skills; or (2) money, either because the owner underestimates how much money it will take to start the business or they are undercapitalized. The following sections will address the first cause and will help you determine whether you have the necessary skills or, if not, how you may be able to acquire them.

Evaluating Your Chances for Success

Once you've decided that you have the right stuff to be an entrepreneur, you're ready to determine whether your business idea has the right stuff. Before you pump your life savings into a small business, you want to know if it has a chance to succeed.

Here's a look at the prime considerations for determining if your business idea has a chance to succeed:

- Market assessment— Is there a market for your product or service? If so, how much income can you expect to derive from it?

- Profitability assessment— How much will starting a new business cost you? Can you afford a lengthy "red ink" period following startup, as well as periodic lulls in cash flow? Can you afford to fail?

- Financing assessment— Will you be able to obtain the necessary financing for your business? If so, from where?

- Legal assessment— What potential legal liabilities are you exposing yourself to by starting a new business? Are the costs of protecting yourself worth the trouble?

- Researching your industry— How can you learn more about your chosen industry and about the resources that are available to help you?

Once you complete these assessments, you will be able to begin to understand the viability of the idea that you have. A closer look at the Free Enterprise Model may help you understand this cycle a little better.

Free Enterprise Model

As I have worked with hundreds of companies over the years, there exists a certain model of basic entrepreneurship, or free enterprise. It consists of three basic principles, with a few subsets, or elements that drive the model. In fact, if you are a business owner or a manager of an enterprise—whether a small, medium or larger enterprise—you can use this model as a valuable tool in moving an idea forward. This model is universal and allows all types of managers in all types of industries to work with an idea and either bring it to fruition or decide to ban the idea.

First, it begins with an IDEA that moves the manager to some form of action. The *idea* begins to take shape as the OPPORTUNITY is sized up and analyzed. The manager then begins to communicate his or her *idea* to others, and conducts further analysis of the *opportunity*. This analysis is required to realize just how viable the *opportunity* may or may not be.

Once it is determined that there exists a fairly practical *opportunity*, the manager then begins to design a plan for gathering the proper RESOURCES. In this case, the *resources* are those elements that are needed to turn an *opportunity* into reality. The *resources* required here may vary from organization to organization, but there are a few basic *resources* to consider: Tools, Technology, Capital, Industry Best Practices, Partners, Suppliers, Value Added Resellers (VARs), and most important People, or staff – not the management team. *Resources* are vastly important in the overall success of making the *opportunity* a reality.

After the Resources have been identified and even allocated, the next step is to formulate the TEAM that will be responsible for driving the entire concept into a formidable, moneymaking *opportunity*. The team is made up of individuals who will be held responsible for the success (or heaven forbid, failure) of the *opportunity*.

Figure 1.1: Free Enterprise Model

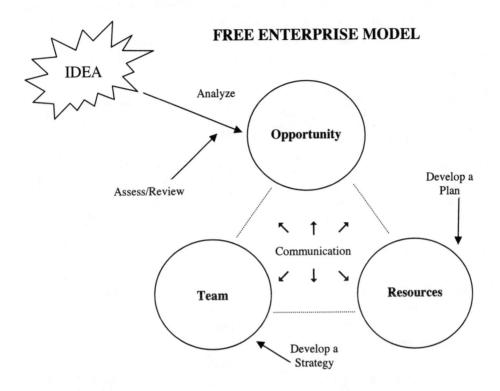

As you go through the exercises of sizing up an opportunity, gathering the proper resources and assembling the best management team, four very important elements should not be overlooked as the process continues. Those four elements are:

- Communication
- Plan of Action
- Strategy
- Assessment/Review

Communication is paramount throughout the entire process. If communication breaks down, the process breaks down and will ultimately fail. Several years ago, I introduced the Power Planning Model for strategic planning, in which I explain that communication is the foundation of all successful planning operations. Pay close attention to the communication between members of the planning committee and management. Keep a close watch that someone is driving the process forward and that no backbiting or undermining is occurring.

Develop a Plan of Action and see the fruits of your planning labors. This is where you will actually begin to *implement* what you have designed. Your Action Plan is your Implementation Strategy.

How will you put into practice what you have committed to writing? Although the Strategic Plan itself is a call to multiple forms of action, a succinct Plan of Action to get things moving is also required. It outlines the steps you will be taking, your milestones you and your team will be achieving, who is responsible for the completion of the milestone, start and end dates, and a budget for each element.

Strategy is defined as **1 a** (1): the science and art of employing the political, economic, psychological, and military forces of a nation or group of nations to afford the maximum support to adopted policies in peace or war (2): the science and art of military command exercised to meet the enemy in combat under advantageous conditions **b**: a variety of or instance of the use of strategy **2 a**: a careful plan or method: a clever stratagem **b**: the art of devising or employing plans or stratagems toward a goal **3**: an adaptation or complex of adaptations (as of behavior, metabolism, or structure) that serves or appears to serve an important function in achieving evolutionary success.

And ***Stratagem*** is defined as **1 a**: an artifice or trick in war for deceiving and outwitting the enemy **b**: a cleverly contrived trick or scheme for gaining an end.

Whether it comes down to war, winning a game or beating your competition, formulating a strategy is the first step to achieving success.

Assessment and Reviews should occur after you have implemented your plan. You will need to assess how well your plan is working. You should review with your team what things are working and which things are not.

Has the plan been implemented? What are the bumps in the road that have occurred? What changes should you make? Who should you reward if things are going well? (Don't forget this item…people like to be recognized for doing a good job.)

We will cover this area in more detail later.

Roles You'll Be Expected to Play

If you're currently employed, you have firsthand knowledge of what it's like to be an employee. If you think going into business for yourself will mostly mean doing the same thing, but for yourself, you're in for a surprise. Small business owners are responsible for the entire business, which involves a lot more than just providing goods or services. It's likely that all the administrative and managerial duties currently performed by your employer will fall on you.

We've all heard of the beleaguered executive who moans that he's overworked because he has to wear two or three hats at his company. Well, most small business owners would give anything if they had to wear *only* two or three hats.

Sales taxes and payroll or self-employment taxes will have to be collected and paid. Accounts receivable and accounts payable will arise in almost any business setting. Providing customer service, keeping the appropriate equipment and supplies in stock, as well as tracking and maintaining inventory and work in progress are activities vital to most businesses. As a new small business owner, it's more than likely there'll be no one except you to do them. And you'll be doing these things *in addition to* the activities that directly relate to providing goods or services to your customers.

The following are some of the roles you can expect to play if you own your own business:

- Tax collector — If you sell goods at the retail level, you're responsible for collecting a sales tax for various government entities; also, if you have employees, you're responsible for paying payroll taxes.

- <u>Manager/boss</u> — If you have employees, you'll be responsible for all of the human resources-related functions, including recruiting, hiring, firing, and keeping track of all the benefits information; you'll be the one filling out all the insurance forms, answering employee questions and complaints, and making the decisions about whether you should change the benefits package you offer your employees.

- <u>Sales/marketing/advertising executive</u> — In addition to having to plan your marketing or advertising campaign, you'll have to carry it out. You may write advertising copy, do some preliminary market research, visit potential customers, and make sure existing customers stay happy. Depending upon the type of business you own, you may have to join business groups; attend various breakfasts, lunches, and dinners; and just generally network with anyone who could help your business prosper.

- <u>Accountant</u> — Even if you have an accountant, you'll have to know basic accounting; in other words, you'll have to know which records to keep and how to keep them. If you don't have an accountant, you'll also have to prepare all of your tax forms, and you'll have to know how to prepare and interpret all of your own financial statements.

- <u>Lawyer</u> — Even if you have a lawyer, you'll have to know basic business law. If you don't have a lawyer, you'll have to prepare all of your own contracts and other documents—and you will need to have a good understanding of the employment laws if you have employees or want to hire someone.

- <u>Business planner</u> — As you own your business, you'll inevitably want to make changes, perhaps to expand the business or add a new product line. If you want to make a change, it'll be your responsibility to do it. You'll have to plan it and execute it, and you'll have to consider all of the ramifications of your decision.

- <u>Bill collector</u> — When customers don't pay, it'll be up to you to collect from them. You'll have to know what you can and can't do when collecting. You'll have to decide how best to collect from them and when to give up.

- <u>Market researcher</u> — Before you start your business, you'll have to find out who your customers are and where they're located. You may also have to conduct market research at various times during the life of your business, such as when you are considering introducing a new product.

- <u>Technology expert</u> — As a small business owner, you will probably come to depend upon your computer. You'll have to get it fixed when it breaks, install upgrades, and load software. You'll also have to keep up with the newest products and the latest changes in technology.

- <u>Clerk/receptionist/typist/secretary</u> — Even if you have clerical help, you'll inevitably do some of your filing, some of your typing, some of your mailing, and some of your telephone answering; even if you have someone else, for example, keep track of overdue accounts, you'll have to know how to do it so that you can teach them what to do.

I included this list of the important responsibilities of running a business so you can realistically start to appraise your chances for success. Obviously, much of your time will be spent on the mechanics of complying with the requirements imposed on you as a business owner. If you're going to succeed, you'll have to do so in the time that remains.

Don't make the mistake of underestimating the cost, in hours, of being in business for yourself. A person who spends 40 hours a week focused on his or her work will have to work a lot more hours as a business owner to get in 40 hours of activity directly relating to providing customers goods or services. And during the startup period, you'll probably be the busiest you've ever been in your lifetime.

EXAMPLE:

A friend of mine decided that he would start a business and focus on marketing various products to the construction industry. He hooked up with a neighbor who had invented a highly concentrated mixture of mortar for applying stucco. As time went on, he quickly realized that he was doing most of the work in running the day-to-day affairs of business, while his new partner basically did nothing to grow the business, let alone run the day-to-day affairs. As you can probably tell, this was a formula for disaster, and the two partners spent their time feuding with one another and lost focus of their original objective…to build a business and generate sales. The business ended, and a lawsuit ensued; and, as in most cases, only the attorneys emerged as winners. The lesson(s) to be learned are numerous in this short example, yet the most prevalent is the fact that the burden of growing and operating a business was shifted to one partner, while the other partner expected things to automatically fall into place, and sit back collect royalties from his invention.

Playing the Role of Leader

As a business owner you will need to dust off your leadership skills and provide a wide array of mature, professional, leadership. You will need to call on those skills as you deal with potential clients; work with vendors; entertain potential investors; and, of course, direct employees.

The following is a list a tracts that a true a true leader should posses. Where you may lack some of these important traits, look to your partners, employees or outside consultants to assist you. One of the things I have found invaluable in my career is to assess your strengths and weaknesses. Use your talents wisely, and find out if you are cut out to be a leader. The following list may help you as you develop leaders in your business…including yourself:

24 Traits of Leadership

1. Leaders Lead by Example without Managing Others

2. Leaders Know Their Followers

3. Leaders Earn the Respect of Their Peers

4. Leaders Have a Vision and Share it with Others

5. Leaders Deal in Honesty and Integrity

6. Leaders Empower Others to Find Success

7. Leaders Control Emotions, Especially Anger

8. Leaders Motivate and Inspire Others

9. Leaders Don't Look for Excuses or Scapegoats When Things Go Wrong

10. Leaders are Able to Adapt when Faced with the Challenges of Change

11. Leaders are Never Happy With the Status Quo and Seek New Adventures

12. Leaders Are Confident in Their Ability to Lead (Or They Fake It Really Well)

13. Through Example, Leaders Earn the Right to Be Heard

14. Leaders Do Not Rationalize Their Weaknesses, They Seek to Turn Them into Strengths

15. Leaders Quickly Change Their Fears to Confidence

16. Leaders Learn To Trust Others

17. Leaders Confront Problems and Look for Fair Solutions

18. Leaders Allow for Two-Way Communication

19. Leaders Learn the Art of Listening Before Engaging Their Mouths

20. Leaders Delegate and Allow Others to Grow

21. Leaders Are Not Afraid of Making Decisions

22. Leaders Possess a Winning Attitude

23. Leaders Demonstrate Professional Courage

24. Leaders Seek for Personal and Team Improvement

Pros and Cons of Owning a Business

Owning a small business is not just another job. It's a totally different lifestyle. You have to ask yourself whether you're ready for a complete commitment to the success of your business. Just as importantly, if you are in a relationship, you should ask your partner whether he or she is completely committed to supporting you in your efforts.

As a small business owner, you're going to have less time for your personal life and you'll probably be using much of what you own as collateral to raise money for the business. If you are willing to make those sacrifices, then let's move on to some of the advantages and disadvantages of owning your own business.

Pros:

- You have the chance to make a lot more money than you can make working for someone else.

- You'll be your own boss and make the decisions that are crucial to your business's success or failure.

- You may be the boss of other people.

- You'll have job security — no one can fire you.

- You'll have the chance to put your ideas into practice.

- You may participate in every aspect of running a business.

- You'll learn more about every aspect of a business and gain experience in a variety of disciplines.

- You'll have the chance to work directly with your customers.

- You'll be able to benefit the local economy, such as by hiring other people to work for you.

- You'll have the personal satisfaction of creating and running a successful business.

- You'll be able to work in a field or area that you really enjoy.

- You'll have the chance to build real retirement value (for example, by selling the business when you retire).

- You'll have the chance to put down roots in a community and to provide a sense of belonging and stability for your family.

Cons:

- You may have to take a large financial risk.

- You will probably have to work long hours and may have fewer opportunities to take vacations.

- You may end up spending a lot of your time attending to the details of running a business and less time on those things you really enjoy.

- You may find that your income is not steady and that there are times when you don't have much income coming in at all.

- You may have to undertake tasks you find unpleasant, such as firing someone or refusing to hire a friend or relative, or collecting receivables.

- You may have to learn many new disciplines, such as filing and bookkeeping, inventory control, production planning, advertising and promotion, market research, and general management.

Specific pros and cons of the home-based business:

- Your startup costs will be lower.

- Your operating costs will be lower than they would be if you were renting space and paying utilities.

- Your commute will be shorter!

- If your location is unimportant to your business, you can theoretically live anywhere and still operate your business.

- You may be more flexible in your schedule if your business can be conducted at your convenience or outside "normal" weekday business hours.

- On the other hand, you're much more vulnerable to interruptions from family members, neighbors, and door-to-door salespeople.

- You may have trouble attracting qualified employees.

- You may be less accessible to suppliers.

- You may worry about your image and about how it "looks" to work from home. However, with the growing popularity of home businesses, such concerns are becoming far less common.

- You may run out of space at home as your business grows.

CHAPTER TWO:
Do You Have What It Takes?

"If a man cannot dream he will soon be asleep to all the important things this life has to offer. If a man cannot pray he will soon only listen to himself. And if he has no charity for others he will soon be the only important thing in his pathetic existence." —Brian Hazelgren

Starting a small business takes a lot of courage. But, as they say, courage doesn't pay the bills. To be successful — to stay in business — you need more than courage. You need a combination of hard work, skill, perseverance, and sometimes old-fashioned luck.

Generally, people who start their own businesses can be grouped into two broad categories. The first group consists of people who know exactly what they want to do and are merely looking for the opportunity or resources to do it. Usually, these people have already developed many of the skills necessary to succeed in their chosen fields. They are also likely to be familiar with industry customs and practices, which can help during the startup phase of a new business.

The second group consists of people who want to start their own business, but don't have any real definite ideas about what they'd like to do. While these people have developed skills in the course of their employment or education, they may not be interested in opening a business in the same field of endeavor.

How you proceed will depend, in large part, on which group you're in. For those who know what they want to do, the task is a bit easier. There's no need to research business ideas and opportunities to decide which might be suitable. Instead, these folks can jump right in and assess their chances for success in the type of business they've selected. Those who merely want out of the traditional corporate world have an extra step: choosing the right small business for you.

In this section, we'll take a closer look at just how much hard work, skill, and perseverance you'll need if you're to be successful. (We can't do much about the luck.) We'll try to give you a sense of what you can expect from a small business, as well as what a small business will expect from you.

To evaluate your own aptitude for small business ownership, you need to:

- Understand the responsibilities of ownership. What's involved in owning a business and what are the roles you'll have to play if you own one? How many hats must you wear as a small business owner? Are you ready to be one of Uncle Sam's sales tax collectors? Are you ready to "manage" your customers? Are you ready to be the boss? This is a good place to start if you're considering starting your own business but haven't owned one before.

- Set your goals. What do you want from your business? If you want to "succeed," how will you know if you get there? Knowing what you want from your business permeates all of the other decisions you'll have to make in starting a new business. It will affect which business you choose, how you evaluate your chances for success, and how you determine if you have the right skills.

- Find out if you have the right stuff. How can you evaluate your own skills and make judgments about whether you're ready to own your own business? This is a good place to start if you already know that you want to own a business.

- Estimate the impact on your everyday life. How will your life change when you become a business owner? Many of the more "secure" aspects of employee life will vanish when you open up your own business.

Can You Handle the Impact on Your Life?

Being self-employed is fundamentally different than being an employee. The distinction between work time and personal time blurs. If a problem arises with the business, it's *your* problem, and it won't go away merely because you've closed the doors for the day. Decisions you make regarding the business will have a direct and immediate impact on your personal life. For example, if you're in retail and decide to remain open evenings, it's your time that's affected. And you're likely to be on call 24 hours a day in the event an emergency arises regarding your business.

The impact is even greater if your business involves working out of your home. You may experience conflicts over the use of space for business or personal purposes. The distinction between your personal life and business life is even further attenuated. Even when you're at home, you're also physically at work. On the upside, there's no commute and you can eat cheaper at home.

If you have a family, it's important to measure the impact opening a new business will have on them. It's best to discuss this as soon as you seriously start to consider the idea. Both you and your family must be willing to put up with the changes owning a business will bring into your lives. Some people experience emotional and physical strain from being on their own and working the hours it takes to make it.

The following aspects of day-to-day living will be seriously affected by your decision to open your own business:

Certainty and source of income. One of the biggest differences between being self-employed and being an employee is the source of your income. Employees can generally expect to receive a paycheck at fixed intervals and for a known amount. (Those working on commission or receiving tips have less certainty regarding the amount.)

As the owner of a new small business, you'll be paid only when and if the business generates enough money. Even successful businesses rarely generate a profit in the beginning stages of operation. You'll have to be prepared for a period during which your expenses will exceed any income derived from the new business.

Health insurance. Although employees are being called upon to pay an increasingly larger share of health insurance costs, it's even tougher for a small business owner. There is no employer to pick up some portion of the premium cost. There's no pool of employees that would allow you to negotiate a more favorable rate than you can get on an individual policy. On the other hand, you may be able to join an association of other small businesses so you can take advantage of less expensive group insurance rates.

Plan now for health insurance needs

For those covered under employer-provided health care plans who leave to start a business, there's the option of continuing coverage through the former employer's plan under the COBRA law. However, you're responsible for the full cost of premiums: The former employer generally won't be contributing anything for you. Also, you're entitled to continued coverage for a limited period of time: as little as 18 months or as long as 36 months, depending on the circumstances. You might be able to get better coverage for the same cost elsewhere. If you are married and your spouse has insurance through an employer plan, consider coverage through that plan.

Retirement savings. Retirement savings are a little different than health insurance. If you don't have health insurance and experience a catastrophic injury or disease, you may be wiped out. The impact of failing to save for your retirement can be even more damaging, but people tend to minimize the risk because "retirement is such a long way off."

Save for retirement

It's no surprise the saving rate is higher among employees than small business owners. Employer-sponsored plans provide a convenient and painless way to set aside a portion of each paycheck. A small business owner has to make a conscious decision to save, outside the framework of a plan administered by someone else. That decision often can be deferred or forgotten when you feel the cash coming in has to be put right back into the business.

Do You Have the Right Stuff?

If asked whether they had the "right stuff" to run a small business, most people who are interested in starting a new business would answer with a resounding "yes." The purpose of this section is not to arrive at a "yes" or a "no" answer; it's really just to help you evaluate your strengths and weaknesses so you'll be in a better position to make certain decisions that you'll have to make before you start a new small business.

There are two distinctly different roles you'll play while preparing to open and run your own small business. Each requires specific skills. On the one hand, you're the person who will be responsible for providing products or services to your customers. This is true whether you have employees or not. On the other hand, you also have to deal with all the activities that relate to running your business. You need to be able to handle both in order to succeed.

Since every business is unique (or should be), the specific skill set needed to provide products or services will vary. Do your best to gauge the scope of activities that make up the business. Be particularly careful not to overlook the less-enjoyable aspects of the business. And every business has a few. Regardless of your desire to go into business for yourself, if you lack needed skills, it's unlikely you'll succeed unless you find a way to compensate.

For example, should you take on partners? Should you hire an accountant or a lawyer? Should you hire a store manager (if you're opening a retail business)? Should you work from home? Your answer to these questions and many others will depend in large part upon which skills you have and which skills you lack.

To begin the process of examining your strengths and weaknesses, select one of the following:

- The first step is assessing your strengths and weaknesses.

- The second step is looking at the personality traits of a successful owner.

- The third step is comparing the two lists and deciding what to do.

- If you already feel that you know your strengths and weaknesses, you can move straight to evaluating your chances for success, which is an evaluation of your business idea, as opposed to an evaluation of yourself.

How to Quantify Your Goals

Quantifying your goals can be a long process. You'll have to gather a lot more information before you're ready to set specific targets. Eventually, you'll probably want to put those goals together in the form of a business plan.

However, before we move on to the process of getting that information, let's take a look at some of the guidelines you should follow when quantifying your goals:

- **Be specific** — Establish targets that can be easily measured, and use numbers as targets whenever possible. For example, you may set a goal of selling your goods or services across a particular number of counties or states, having a certain number of employees, or reaching a particular level of sales. Tie those numbers to specific time frames (within six months, within two years, within 10 years, etc.).

- **Be realistic** — Having high expectations is great, but make sure that you establish targets that are reasonable and potentially achievable. If you're opening a fast-food restaurant, to say that you want to be bigger than McDonald's within six months is not realistic.

- **Be aggressive** — You can be realistic and still aim high. Don't set goals that are too easily achieved; also, set both short-term and long-term goals. If, after six months in business, you accomplish all of your goals, then what? Don't sell yourself short; if you want to be bigger than McDonald's within 20 years, go for it.

- **Be consistent** — Beware of inadvertently setting inconsistent goals. For example, a goal of growing fast enough to have three employees within two years might be inconsistent with a goal of earning a particular amount of money if the cost of adding the employees ends up temporarily reducing your income below the target level. There is nothing wrong with having both goals. Just be aware that the potential conflict exists, and establish priorities among your goals so that you'll know which ones are most important to you.

Smart Tip:

In developing your goals and objectives, you should be specific where achievements can be measured. Normally you would have a numbered list of a few selected objectives. Keep your list to about 10, because long lists make it hard to focus.

Making your goals concrete is the best way, possibly the only way, to tell when you've achieved them. Your chance of implementation depends on your being able to track progress toward goals and measure results, and implementation is critical. Set measurable objectives such as sales or sales growth, profits or profitability, market share as published by an objective and accessible source, gross margin as percent of sales, for example.

Avoid listing vague goals that can't be tracked. Where general or intangible goals are important to your business, find a way to make them specific. For example, if customer satisfaction is a priority, put your objectives in terms of percent of returns, specific numbers of complaints, or letters of praise, or some other measure related to satisfaction. If image or awareness is a priority, include a survey to measure the change in percentages in your plan. You can build a customer satisfaction survey into your plan, set the sample size and satisfaction scores you want to achieve, then carry out the survey to check on success.

If you deal with products, you might watch gross margin or unit sales, so you should set objectives for these key factors. If you are a distribution company, for example, then you will also want to focus on tight management of logistics, working capital, and personnel costs. If you are a publisher, then you might focus on product quality, titles, or marketing. This obviously depends on your type of business.

Example of
Goals and Objectives

1. Achieve a 10% response rate on our direct mail and email campaigns.
2. Convert 10% of the responses and bump this number to 12% after Year 2.
3. Operate a highly successful enterprise that continues to provide superior products.
4. Achieve the Sales projections outlined in our business plan.
5. Borrow $500,000 for the expansion of the enterprise and new products, as well as have commitments for capital for acquisitions.
6. Provide an exit strategy for all stakeholders after 2009.
7. Continue to develop new products that enhance the lifestyle of our customers.
8. Build a successful distributor channel with worldwide presence.
9. Achieve a Gross Profit Margin of 65% or greater.
10. Achieve projected milestones, as outlined in our business plan.
11. Have our products in 5,000 retail outlets by 2008.
12. Create jobs in rural areas close to the manufacturing and sales facilities as listed in our Personnel Plan

For a comprehensive and closer look at developing Goals & Objectives, please refer to page 188, Appendix E.

Real Life Goals

EXAMPLE:

James was a general contractor for most of his adult life. At the age of 60 he decided that he wanted to create a business that would provide jobs for his children and grandchildren. He did this because it would create an income that they could provide for their families if they chose to stay in the business.

Growing up as a poor farm boy, James did not want his family to be submitted to or even experience poverty—or a lack of income as he had. His goal was to be able to provide a way for his family to work and enjoy making a living, yet at the same time have a little ownership in a small business. He took out a second mortgage on his home, leveraged everything he owned, and started a real estate business; not just any real estate business, but one that required skills in multi-family units or apartments.

Since James was a general contractor who was very familiar with the construction business, he became the owner and general contractor to build the apartment complexes. In the beginning he built 112 apartments complete with a community swimming pool, clubhouse for tenants to relax, and a beautiful center courtyard that the entire complex was built around. This first attempt of owning and operating multi-family real estate proved to be a profitable venture for the family, and it became very successful.

After a few years in running this business James and his children decided that another apartment complex could be built adjacent to the first complex and they began to develop the plans for an additional 132 units. This thriving real estate business provided the jobs for his children and grandchildren for many years. It was a dream come true, and the business and James were blessed with much success.

The initial dream of owning and operating a thriving business to create jobs for his children and grandchildren was not only realized but was a tremendous boost to the entrepreneurial drive of his children and grandchildren.

Getting started. Some people have a hard time setting goals because they just don't know where to start. If this applies to you, try this simple exercise designed to help you get focused on your goals and objectives.

Start with an easily quantifiable goal. Then list the amount of money you'll need to earn in order to cover your living expenses since, no matter what, you'll need to make enough to make ends meet. Only when you have met that need can you begin to look to other goals.

Fill out the *Top 10 Goals Worksheet* and read the article, *"Discover the Work You Were Born to Do,"* included in the Appendix.

To help you even further about who you are and what you want out of life, move to the next section and complete the worksheet *Things About Me*. This worksheet will assist you in developing a clearer picture of what makes you "tick", and what drives you to accomplish things. It is a self-assessment that will require a little thought and complete honesty.

Things About Me Worksheet

Complete the following self-assessment worksheet as honestly as you can. Just write down whatever comes to mind; don't over think the exercise. Most likely, your first response will be your best. Once you have finished the exercise, look for patterns (i.e., is there a need for a business doing one of the things you like or are good at?)

1. List at least five things you like to do or are good at.

_____

_____

_____

_____

_____

2. List five things you are not good at or you don't like to do.

_____

_____

_____

_____

_____

3. If there were three products or services that would make your personal life better, what would they be?

    _____

    _____

    _____

4. If there were three products or services that would make your business life better, what would they be?"

    _____

    _____

    _____

5. When people ask what you do, what's your answer? (List one occupation or whatever mainly occupies your week.)

    _____

    _____

    _____

6. List three things you enjoy about your work.

    _____

    _____

    _____

7. List three things you dislike about your work.

    _____

    _____

    _____

8. When people tell you what they like most about you, what do they say?

    _____

    _____

    _____

9. How would you respond to the following: "Some people dislike the fact that I"?

    _____

    _____

    _____

10. Other than your main occupation, list any other skills you possess, whether you excel at them or not.

_____

_____

_____

_____

_____

11. In addition to becoming more financially independent, what else would you like more of?

_____

_____

_____

_____

_____

12. Write down three things you want to see changed or improved about your community.

_____

_____

_____

13. Write down three things you would like to change about yourself.

_____

_____

_____

14. If the world were perfect, what would your world look like or include?

_____

_____

_____

_____

15. List the top five reasons you want to go into business for yourself.

_____

_____

_____

_____

_____

Choosing a Type of Business

Most of the books you read on the subject of finding a small business will tell you that the best place to start is with a matching of your skills and experiences to some business that requires those skills. For example, if you love to cook, they'll suggest you open a catering business or a restaurant.

If you have a strong interest in something, think about the needs of other people who share your interests. This is important as you build your business because you should maintain a relatively optimistic outlook and have a burning passion for operating a small business. If there are needs to be filled, you should be the one to do it. So, is there some type of product of service that you can provide? It may help to think in terms of *goods* and *services*. Most businesses involve a mixture of both, but this discussion may help narrow the focus.

Ultimately, considering doing something you love is a start, but it has to be further analyzed by examining the market potential, competition, resources required to enter the market (tools, technology, people and capital), consumer/buyer demand, and uniqueness of the idea. By balancing enthusiasm with reality, you should be able to come up with the business that fits you and your passion…at the same time meeting and fulfilling a market demand.

Work Smart

The best place to start in picking a small business is with consumers (including other businesses that may want your product or service). What do consumers or businesses want that's not being provided to them? Ultimately, whether you succeed will depend upon whether you are able to meet some unmet need in the market.

If you love to cook, you're more likely to succeed if you start a landscaping business— even if you know nothing about landscape design — than you are if you open a catering service…*if there is a demand for landscape design services but not for another catering company in your area.* It's far easier to hire someone who knows something about landscaping than it is to sell consumers something that they don't want or need.

Of course, you don't necessarily have to sell a new or different product or service in order to succeed; you can succeed if you can improve what is already being sold. In the above example, you could open a catering business if you can provide a better service than other catering businesses, such as a wider menu or lower prices. But that's *still* a function of what consumers want. Your research would have told you that there is a demand for a new catering business if prices were lower or if the menu were more varied.

Now that you have an idea of what you need, here's how to get it:

A comprehensive study and analysis of all your potential markets is something most small business owners either don't know how to do themselves because they lack the training or can't afford to pay someone else to do because it's so expensive. But there are a few less expensive (and, admittedly, less scientifically exact) techniques that you can use to find out what consumers want.

Once you have some idea of what the market wants, *now* is the time to begin looking at your skills and experiences. You'll need to match your skills with what the market wants. Once you match your skills to what's available, you should be well on your way to picking the small business that's right for you.

As we all know, a lot of new small businesses fail each year. In most of those cases, the small business owners were probably convinced that their idea for a business was a perfect match for their skills. They were wrong. You can learn from their errors and avoid the mistakes they made. You can learn from my errors, and the mistakes that I have made over the past two decades. In fact, there are some common mistakes that many failed small businesses make. I have had to learn from my own experiences on successes as well as failures.

Think about it for a minute…every business has had failures. Even something as simple as changing a color in your logo can be considered a failure… because something else replaced it. Which leads into a brief discussion on *the success that can come from failure*.

The Success in Failure

Behind every successful person is a legacy of past failures. Consider Abraham Lincoln who suffered defeat in four elections before being voted in as President. Babe Ruth struck out 1,330 times on his way to hitting 714 homers. He also hit a record 60 home runs in the 1927 season. Then, there is Tom Monaghan who failed in business twice before launching Domino's Pizza.

Failure hurts, traumatizes and can even destroy one's ego, but it also challenges, motivates and humbles people…cutting right through the false impression that success is easy to obtain.

Avis Rent a Car founder, Warren Avis, gives a little advice about failure. This comes after years of business experience.

- There is no such thing as the perfect deal. Look for what is wrong with it.

- Despite popular opinion to the contrary, the first solution to a problem is usually not the best. Force yourself to list at least four other solutions…because 80 percent of the time one of them will be better than your original solution.

- If properly put together, groups make better decisions than individuals. Take advantage of the talents others possess… especially the oddball who sees things a little differently.

- Expect the unexpected—more often than not, it happens. Be prepared for the worst.

- Never say never.

*Source: Entrepreneur Press

Many entrepreneurs believe that failure is essential to long-term success. "The more you fail the more you succeed," maintains Karl Mason, author of *Using Intelligent Fast Failure.*

To develop "intelligent failure"—the type that Mason says forms building blocks to success – the first step is to get over the fear of failure. We are constantly dealing with failure. If you find something not working, you try something else…that means the first thing has failed. Or, that there is something better and you need to find out what it is.

Job seekers line up dozens of interviews because they know most of them will result in rejection. Sales people call on dozens of people because they know most of them will say no. Inventors know they will fail many times over before they come upon the magic formula that will eventually work.

Mason suggests a term called STRAFFING…*Success Through Rapid Accelerated Failure*. He suggests that entrepreneurs put together many ideas and try them out quickly to see which ones work. In other words, try out many ideas at the same time. This greatly accelerates the learning process and compresses failure time, allowing you to progress more rapidly toward a solution. Each idea will possess some positive elements that will combine with other positive elements of things/ideas discarded—to form a new solution.

It's no secret that creativity is crucial to the success of any entrepreneur. Business owners need to constantly address new ideas and develop new ways of looking at problems or situations. This was made evident at a conference on failure at the University of Michigan. Participants were asked to build the tallest structure they could, using only notched ice cream sticks. The results offered some insight into different ways of learning from failure:

- Some participants persisted in building the same type of structure despite repeated collapses, while other participants altered their designs, trying out different approaches. Typically, people who tried different options were able to build higher structures.

- Some participants peeked at what others were building and borrowed (or stole) their ideas. This can be great way to leapfrog technology. There's no sense in reinventing the wheel every time.

- Other people worked in groups to pool resources. Groups can capitalize on each other's ideas and share in the success (or the blame if the venture is a flop).

The key is learning from our errors as we go so that small failures do not become big ones. To learn from experience, including past mistakes, we need accurate perceptions and honest self-appraisal. While denial may heal the wounds failure inflicts on our egos, the successful entrepreneur spends quite a bit of time analyzing his or her mistakes and finding innovative ways to profit from them.

Put things in the best possible perspective and learn the most useful lesson possible. Work quickly to get out from under your failures and into your best frame of mind. This is where problems yield solutions.

You will find yourself often wondering why you decided to take on being an entrepreneur. You will experience setbacks…it is part of life…moving on is the key. Ask yourself "What is the lesson in this setback?" Be honest with yourself. And then ask, "Where is the opportunity?" Find the opportunity. Think it through, and come up with a solution.

Don't beat yourself up emotionally about setbacks or the past; use them to change the future. As an entrepreneur you will need to have (or develop) a high sense of tolerance to failure. It is inevitable that you will fail at something…even multiple things. Learn from it and move on.

Sometimes an attitude adjustment is needed in dealing with stress and pressures. Bad things happen to good people, but often there is a big difference in reality and your perception of it. When tense moments creep into your life, ask yourself, "Is this really a crisis, or am I making a mountain out of a molehill?"

Think about this…reality must be balanced with a courageous sense of vision and perseverance.

> **Did you know: Thomas Edison failed over 1,000 times before creating the light bulb!**

For those who listen, setbacks are good teachers. (If you don't listen you are doomed to experience the real definition of insanity…doing the same thing over and over and over, and expecting a different result.) Mix it up a bit. Try something a little different. Thomas Edison failed over a thousand times before he invented the light bulb. He kept trying something a little different each time. Besides honing your business skills, setbacks can also develop an inner resiliency. Those who fail are more likely to see the bigger picture, take the lesson to be learned from the failure and try to incorporate those lessons into their daily life in business as well as personally. As a result, these individuals are less likely to be disturbed by daily pressures. They quickly learn not to sweat the small stuff, but to focus their energy and talents on solving the bigger problems.

Do entrepreneurs learn more from setbacks than from successes? One entrepreneur has figured out an important element of success and failure: "Success is a reward for hard work—not a teacher. It is the hard lessons that I learned along the way that led to my success."

Have you seen the inspiring commercial that Michael Jordan did for Nike? It's the one where he talks about all of his mistakes, such as the free throws and game-deciding shots that he's missed over the years. I love that commercial for its right attitude about failure, but I'm even more impressed with it after seeing a follow-up interview with Jordan.

A reporter asked Michael Jordan if the statistics that he quoted in the commercial were correct. Jordan's response? "I don't know."

Now that answer surprised me at first, until I realized its significance: Michael Jordan is so unconcerned with failure that he truly has no idea how many shots he's missed in his career or how many games have been lost because of his mistakes. He simply took the word of the statisticians at Nike for those numbers.

Like Jordan, we all fail. Success isn't based on "avoiding" failure, but on "facing" it correctly. William A. Ward said, "Failure should be our teacher, not our undertaker. Failure is delay, not defeat. It is a temporary detour, not a dead-end street."

Successful leaders don't avoid failure. They "handle" it --successfully. If you spend much time worrying about failure, you, too, increase your chances of taking a fall.

TREAT FAILURES AS FRIENDS, NOT ENEMIES

Elbert Hubbard said, "Constant effort and frequent mistakes are the stepping-stones of genius." Failures can be great learning experiences. As a leader, I believe I've had more failures than most people. But I've also had many successes. Why? Because, to me, "trying" is more important than "not failing." And when I do make mistakes, I use them as learning experiences, asking, "What did I do wrong, and how can I do it better next time?"

Don't try to hide your mistakes. Admit them, and then learn and grow from them. Since you will have failures, why not treat them as the friends they can be?

HAVE SUCCESSFUL FAILURES, NOT FAILED SUCCESSES

With each setback, Lincoln continued to persevere and learn from his mistakes. Rather than being a failure at success, he experienced successful failures. The experiences didn't stop him; they taught him. Four failed attempts made his more resolute to succeed. How many times will you make mistakes along your journey as an entrepreneur? I don't have a definite number to offer you, but what I can assure you is that you should plan on making mistakes, and even failing. Successful failures can be excellent teachers and provide you with sound advice on how not to do it the next time around.

SEE FAILURES AS FRESH OPPORTUNITIES, NOT FINAL DEFEATS

When shipwrecked on Malta, the Apostle Paul ministered to the people. When arrested, he saw it as a chance to preach the Gospel. As he said, "My dear friends, I want you to know that what has happened to me has helped to spread the good news" (Phil. 1:12, CEV).

When our attitudes are right, failure actually helps and improves us. It gives us a chance to see where we fall short, to change, and to learn more about ourselves and how we can grow to our maximum potential.

"Failing to try" is the greatest failure anyone can experience. If we don't make the attempt, we cannot succeed. A very good example of this can be seen in the life of the baseball great, Ty Cobb. In 1915, he set what was then the all-time record for stolen bases in a season with 96 steals. Seven years later, Max Carey set the second-best record with 51 stolen bases. Amazingly, Carey failed only 2 times in 53 attempts. Cobb failed 38 times in his 134 attempts. I suspect that if Carey had tried more times, he would have had more failures, but he may have been the one to set the record that would be unbeaten today!

As leaders, as entrepreneurs, we must be less like Carey and more like Cobb. We must make the attempt and become the best we can at whatever God is calling us to do. We will only do that if we put failure in the proper perspective. So, let's start establishing some goals and objectives, and move into the next discussion.

What Are Your Goals?

Why is it that you want to start a small business? Money? Fame? Personal freedom? Ego gratification? Retirement income? Inability to get rehired or retrained? Discomfort with larger organizations? If someone were to ask you why you're going into business for yourself, what would you say?

For many people, it helps to translate their expectations and desires into concrete terms by setting goals.

Short-term goals. While it's good to have long-term goals, such as becoming independently wealthy and enjoying tons of leisure time, you also need to set short-term goals. Your short-term goals should be realistic and achievable. Some short-terms goals might be to (1) select a name for your business, (2) obtain a business license, (3) find a good small-business lawyer, or (4) establish a business credit card account.

Long-term goals. Long-term goals are also important, giving you something to continue to work toward. Long-term goals typically fall into one of the following three broad categories:

> ➢ **Economic Goals** - For many entrepreneurs, this is a strong inducement. The opportunity to increase personal earnings and achieve their financial potential is often a powerful motivation in starting a business.

➤ **Personal Goals** - Unlike money, many of these factors can't be quantified but are important nevertheless. For many people, the chance to build something of their own, according to their own vision, is what drives them to start a business.

➤ **Retirement Goals** - It's vital for everyone, employee and entrepreneur alike, to recognize there'll come a time when they want to kick back and enjoy the fruits of their labors. In this time of growing concern over the continued viability of the Social Security system, any goal setting you do should involve consideration of your needs *after* you've built and run your business.

If you're still a little uncertain about goals and what they might mean to you, you should take a look at:

- **Why goals are important**

- **How to quantify your goals**

It'll be important psychologically in those chaotic first months to be able to feel that you're making some progress. Short-term goals can help you achieve those small but crucial victories.

Why Goals Are Important

Goals are important because they will affect just about everything you do as you plan and operate your business. Goals are not just the destination you're driving toward; they're also the painted white lines that keep you on the road.

You have a job that pays you $35,000. You hate your job and yearn to leave. You have an idea for a small business that involves servicing a small niche market, and you set a goal of being recognized as the expert in that niche area within five years.

You analyze your idea and discover that while no one else is servicing that market, it's a small market and you're not likely to make more than $32,000 for at least the first three years. Yet, you also discover that because your business is unique and your chances of becoming a recognized expert are good, you'll have much greater income potential after the first three years. Despite the cut in income for three years, you decide the risks are worth it and that you'll start the new business.

Of course, goals won't just determine whether you start a small business, they'll also play a prominent role in just about every decision you make along the way, from how you structure your business planning to whether you hire employees to how you sell and market your product or services.

Once you have some idea of what your general goals are, the next step is to make those goals concrete by quantifying them. It's not enough just to say, for example, that you want to change professions or that you want to be your own boss. You'll need to develop specific targets by quantifying your goals.

Fill out the Top 10 Goals Worksheet in the Appendix

CHAPTER THREE:
Targeting Your Market

Who Is Your Target Buyer?

Do you know precisely who your customers are? You may know many of them by name, but do you really know what type of people or businesses they are? For example, if you sell to consumers, do you have *demographic information* (i.e., what are their average income ranges, education, typical occupations, geographic location, family makeup, etc.) that identifies your target buyer?

What about *lifestyle information* (i.e., hobbies, interests, recreational/ entertainment activities, political beliefs, cultural practices, etc.) on your target buyer?

This type of information can help you in two very important ways. It can help you make changes to your product or service itself, in order to better match with what your customers are likely to want. It can also tell you how to reach your customers through advertising, promotions, etc.

For an obvious example, a company that sells athletic shoes may know that its typical customer is also a sports fan. Thus, if that company can build shoes good enough to be worn by professional athletes; it will have a convincing story about quality to tell. It can also benefit by using well-known athletes as spokespersons in its advertising, and by placing advertisements in sports magazines where its customers are likely to see them.

How can you refine your understanding of your own customer base? I suggest you look at the issue from two angles:

Niche marketing— identifying the heavy users of your product so you can direct your marketing efforts more precisely to those users

Segmenting the market— dividing the existing market up into sections or segments that may become new niches for your business

Niche Marketing

Most marketers know that "20 percent of buyers consume 80 percent of product volume." If you could identify that key 20 percent and find others like them, you could sell much more product with much less effort.

The "heavy users" of your product can be thought of as a market "niche" that you should attempt to dominate. Niche marketing today means targeting, communicating with, selling to, and obtaining feedback from the heaviest users of your business's products or services.

Picking the right segment of the market is important to achieving sufficiently large sales volume and profitability to survive and prosper as a company. Picking the right market segment means that it is:

- Made up of consumers who will buy from you

- Measurable in quantitative terms

- Substantial enough to generate planned sales volume

- Accessible to your company's distribution methods

- Sensitive to planned/affordable marketing spending events

In identifying your niche and the segment of the market you will target, it is also important to examine other factors that could affect your company's success. You will want to consider:

- Strength of competitors to attract your niche buyers away from your products

- Similarity of competitive products in the buyers' minds

- Rate of new product introductions by competitors

- Ease of entry/protectability in the market for your niche

Perhaps the driving force behind "niche" marketing or "segmentation" is the need to satisfy and keep those consumers who really love your products or services. Consumers become increasingly more sophisticated and demanding. And product choices continue to expand with prosperity and global competition.

Even large companies have embraced niche marketing, continuing to refine and target their product offerings to different buyer groups. As an example, Nike restaged a multi-billion dollar company that had plateaued by pursuing a segmentation strategy. Nike designed and marketed athletic shoes for each different sport, often further segmenting with specialized models within each sport (i.e., "Air Jordan" basketball shoes, additional basketball models called "Force," represented by Charles Barkley and David Robinson, and "Flight," represented by Scottie Pippin).

In addition to the considerations listed above, it also is important to be able to identify and estimate the size of your target market, particularly if you're thinking about a new venture, so that you can tell if the customer base is large enough to support your business or new product idea. Remember that it's not enough that people like your business concept. There must be enough target buyers on a frequent-enough basis to sustain your company sales, spending, and profits from year to year.

For example, selling a product or service that people may need only once in a lifetime (i.e., an indestructible pair of shoes) may not be a sustainable business, unless a large number of people need it at any given time, or everyone needs it eventually (i.e., funeral services), or your profit margins generate a substantial income.

How to Segment Your Market

If the universe of all potential buyers is your "market," then the market can be divided up into sections or "segments" based on any number of factors. For example, you might divide up your customers by age group and find that you sell most of your products to people aged 18 to 34. You might divide them up by family size and find that you sell most of your products to married couples with young children. You might divide them up by economic status and find that you sell most products to people with an annual income of about $50,000 to $75,000. You may even divide them up by geographic location and find that you sell most of your products to people living within two specific ZIP codes.

Many small businesses stop there, thinking they have enough information to be able to identify and communicate with their most likely customers. However, larger companies will attempt to push on further and find out even more information about their customers' lifestyles, values, life stage, and so forth.

Let's define some terms:

> **Demographics** refers to age, sex, income, education, race, martial status, size of household, geographic location, size of city, and profession.
>
> **Psychographics** refers to personality and emotionally based behavior linked to purchase choices; for example, whether customers are risk-takers or risk-avoiders, impulsive buyers, etc.
>
> **Lifestyle** refers to the collective choice of hobbies, recreational pursuits, entertainment, vacations, and other non-work time pursuits
>
> **Belief and value systems** include religious, political, nationalistic, and cultural beliefs and values.
>
> **Life stage** refers to chronological benchmarking of people's lives at different ages (i.e., pre-teens, teenagers, empty-nesters, etc.).

How can you find out more about your customers? Through market research, of course. Larger companies segment their markets by conducting extensive market research projects, consisting of several rounds of exploratory research.

Customer and product data collection: Researchers gather data from users of similar products regarding:

- Consumable products, and how often they are consumed
- Number and timing of brand purchases
- Reasons for purchases
- Consumers' attitudes about various product attributes
- Importance of the product to the lifestyle of consumer

- Category user information (demographics, psychographics, media habits, etc.)

- Seasonal uses, and seasonal colors

Factor and cluster analysis: Researchers analyze the data collected in ways to find correlations between product purchases and other factors, as a basis for identifying actionable consumer target "clusters." Clusters are defined as "niche markets," where there are identifiable numbers of buyers or users who share the same characteristics and who thus can be reached by adept advertising and promotion.

Cluster identification and importance ranking: Researchers then determine whether clusters are large and viable enough to spend marketing funds on them whether potential marketing niche clusters fit strategic company objectives; i.e., does marketing to this group fit your existing image and long-term goals?

What can smaller companies do to segment their markets?

Smaller companies can research secondary data sources and conduct individual interviews with key trade buyers and consumers or end users of their products and services (qualitative research). Often qualitative research can be accomplished for free or little expense.

Smaller companies also can conduct informal factor and cluster analysis by:

- Watching key competitors' marketing efforts and copying them

- Talking to key trade buyers about new product introductions

- Conducting needs analyses from qualitative research with individuals and groups

In many cases, smaller companies have access to the same databases as large companies for estimating the sizes of market segment clusters and their importance. Some low-cost sources of external secondary data include:

- Trade and association publications and experts

- Basic research publications

- External measurement services (large market research firms include ACNielsen, Burke, and Information Resources, Inc. (IRI)

- Government publications

Smaller companies can segment markets by geography, distribution, price, packaging, sizes, product life, and other tangible factors in addition to demographics and lifestyle and psychographic clustering. Service businesses will want to go as far as developing a cluster of clients based on a radius within a certain geographical area. For example, an interior designer may want to focus on a 50-mile radius, and a math tutor may look at a 20-mile radius for servicing customer needs. Some service businesses like dry cleaners will even tighten down the radius to about 3 to 5 miles. You decide how large the radius around your business should be, but put some type of limits to where you are physically capable of servicing your customer's needs.

Secondary Market Research

Secondary research is something every student has completed at one time or another, usually by doing library research with books and periodicals for a school report. This is usually the cheapest and easiest type of research for small businesses to conduct. However, it may be less reliable than primary research because the information you obtain is more general as it was not developed with your particular problem or situation in mind.

Nevertheless, for some types of information (for example, questions about your competitor's market share or the absolute numbers of potential customers for a new product), secondary market research is the only kind available.

Secondary research can be divided into two categories:

- **External research**, which involves looking at data gathered by industry experts, trade associations, or companies that specialize in gathering and compiling data about various industries

- **Internal research**, which is data gathered by your company for purposes other than market research (i.e., sales reports broken down by product line) but which you can use to gauge what the market will do in the future

Basically, when you enlist Secondary Research, you are taking a closer look at other opinions and experiences to assist you in formulating your own strategies. (More detail on Secondary Research is provided in Chapter Six).

Your Unique Selling Advantage

In order to be successful at marketing, every business owner needs to focus on what's special and different about his or her business. The best way to do this is to try to express this uniqueness in a single statement.

Rosser Reeves was the author of the phrase, "unique selling proposition," or USP, which is a unique message about a company versus the competition, which each business or brand should develop and use consistently in its advertising and promotion. Although the concept is virtually the same, I have changed the phrase just a bit and call it a "Unique Selling Advantage," or USA. By USA I don't necessarily mean a slogan or a phrase that will appear in your advertising, although that's one possible use for it. However, at this point, we're focusing on its usefulness as a tool to help *you* focus on what your business is all about.

If you cannot concisely describe the uniqueness of your idea (and create some excitement in potential users), you may not have the basis for a successful business.

There are several questions to ask yourself about your business in order to determine a USA:

- What is unique about your business or brand versus direct competitors? You'll probably find a whole list of things that set you apart; the next questions will help you decide on which of these you should focus.

- Which of these factors are most important to the buyers and end users of your business or brand?

- Which of these factors are not easily imitated by competitors?

- Which of these factors can be easily communicated and understood by buyers or end users?

- Can you construct a memorable message (USA) of these unique, meaningful qualities about your business or brand?

- Finally, how will you communicate this message (USA) to buyers and end users? Marketing tools to communicate USAs include media advertising, promotion programs (i.e., direct mail), packaging, and sales personnel.

For examples of USAs, think about different brands of products you've seen advertised on TV. What is the main message underlying the ad? Different brands and types of products utilize different primary themes, attributes, or ideas associated with each brand. For example, cigarette, liquor, and perfume advertising tends to sell brands based on emotional, "borrowed values," instead of strictly product features. Users are encouraged to fantasize that they may accrue the "benefits" of sex appeal or of a more satisfying/fun lifestyle, perhaps portrayed by the famous or beautiful spokespersons for a particular brand.

Food products may also utilize borrowed values in addition to describing product features and benefits. However, products like medicinal brands (i.e., cough and cold products) work hard at identifying and promoting unique features that will provide more relief faster than their competitors' products will. For these types of products, the way the product works is the most meaningful factor for customers.

Home builders also work off of your emotions to sell the product that will make you look good to your neighbors and friends; provide a safe haven for your family; or be conveniently close to work, schools, and shopping. They will even hit the financial nerve again to tell you that your home is your biggest investment, and that you will want to choose a builder that will provide you with the very best value for your money.

The simple test of determining whether you've constructed a good USA for your business is whether it sells for you! If it sells your business or brand, your USA is meaningfully different. If you've been in business for a while, you may have constructed a USA unconsciously. For example, if you decided to provide free delivery service to your customers because no one else in town is doing it, you've constructed a USA based on service that you are communicating to the intended target buyer. If, however, you offer free delivery service because *everyone else* in town does so and you need to provide it simply to keep up with the competition, it's not something that sets you apart and should not be the focus of your USA.

For many small businesses, packaging, sales materials, and sales personnel may be the only marketing tools affordable. For others, it may be that their products are hand crafted and painstakingly assembled with the very best of care. Finally, it is very important to clearly determine your USA to communicate with these limited means.

What's Your Unique Business Idea?

Intuitively, (based on sound research) you believe your business will succeed because you are doing something *different* from some or all of your competitors. The first test of any business, small or large, is its uniqueness when compared to its competitors.

Now, that doesn't mean you can't borrow a good idea from some other source and build a successful business around it. For example, every town needs a certain number of dry cleaning operations, and most of them look very much alike. However, if you examine the more successful dry cleaners in your area, you'll notice that each one tends to emphasize and promote something special. It may be lower prices, faster service, better cleaning, a drive-up window, or more frequent coupons in the local shopping news. Some of these business owners undoubtedly borrowed their marketing ideas from other companies they've dealt with, or from promotions they many have noticed when traveling in other cities. The point is, successful businesses find ways to make their products or services stand out from the crowd, or at least the crowd in their immediate geographic area that is their target.

If your business provides a product, sources of uniqueness can range from pricing, packaging, distribution method, or feature differences, to the mere perception of a difference that may or may not exist. For example, granulated white sugar is difficult to differentiate from one supplier to another except in pricing, packaging, or amount of advertising. But white sugar substitutes like aspartame (i.e., Nutrasweet brand) or saccharine (i.e., Sweet 'n Low brand) have important product feature and benefit differences that help determine consumer purchase decisions.

TIP:

> **Features** are "descriptions" of a product or service (i.e., green color, pear-shaped, inexpensive, fast, slow, etc.)
>
> **Benefits** are the "advantages" you receive from using the product or service (i.e., feel better, look beautiful, more endurance, etc.)

There are two main issues to consider here:

1. How is your business different?

2. Can you express it in terms of a concise statement, known as a "unique selling proposition" or USA, that will form the basis for all your advertising, promotions, sales communications, and other marketing activities?

Is this a difference that customers appreciate, so that they'll prefer or even seek out your business's offerings rather than your competitors?

Do Customers Value Your Uniqueness?

One of the quickest ways to go out of business is to market a product or service that hardly anyone wants, needs, understands, or cannot afford. Find out if there is a *real need* for your idea. *Who and how many people will pay for it, and how much will they pay?*

Ideally, you should always research and test your idea against the realities of the marketplace. Many business owners have tested their ideas by working as employees in their industry for a number of years and have seen firsthand what works and what doesn't. Yet, even well-seasoned industry experts can benefit from analyzing the market environment in a way that will help to evaluate the potential of an idea.

If you are just starting out and are not sure of what business to look into, look for anomalies in the marketplace that you can capitalize on (preferably something that you know about and are interested in). *Webster's Dictionary* defines anomaly as, "departure from the...usual method; abnormality," in other words, something out of the ordinary.

In marketing terms, an "anomaly" is an unsatisfied need that you can use to make a profit.

EXAMPLE:

Before Federal Express came into being, a great number of business people wished there was an affordable way to send important packages and documents overnight. However, the tremendous startup costs (over $500 million) and logistics problems (coordinating a national fleet of trucks and planes to start business on the first day) made it seem an impossible dream, until Federal Express showed the world how to do it.

Now there are over a dozen different international companies that specialize in sending packages and documents anywhere overnight! Once the United States market had matured at around $14 billion per year, aggressive international service and marketing has grown the express "overnight" package delivery service to a $30 billion business today. The "anomaly" was the great unsatisfied need for overnight package delivery that everyone thought was impossible to do.

In order to be able to accurately determine whether your business idea has enough appeal to a sufficient number of customers, you'll have to become very aware of who your target buyers are.

So how do you effectively evaluate ideas that you are considering? Should you hire a marketing firm to help you sort this out? Perhaps, down the road; but, for now, consider a simple checklist that will assist you to make an intelligent decision. I realize that might be a stretch for some…to make an "intelligent decision," but even the most pigheaded and naïve can come up with the proper formula for deciding whether to move forward with a concept or new enterprise.

The next phase of this discussion encompasses an important model known as the Checklist for Evaluating Ideas. I purposely wanted to include this checklist because I couldn't find it to be a good tool for analyzing a product or service. It goes hand in hand with the Free Enterprise Model that was introduced earlier. Because after all, the first concept in evaluating the validity of an opportunity is to first come up with the IDEA. So, go through the Checklist for Evaluating Ideas and find out if there really is an opportunity waiting for you out there. Good luck!

Checklist for Evaluating Business Ideas

☐ Have you considered all the advantages or benefits of the idea? Is there a real need for it? What are the needs you can think of?

☐ Have you pinpointed the exact problems or difficulties your idea is expected to solve? What are they?

☐ Is your idea original, a new concept, or is it a new combination or adaptation? What made you decide to come up with this new concept?

☐ What immediate or short-range gains or results can be anticipated? Are the projected returns adequate?

☐ Name the risk factors you think are associated with your idea. Are the risk factors acceptable? (Be honest here, and closely evaluate the risks you are taking on).

☐ What long-range benefits can be anticipated in terms of satisfaction, revenue, corporate identity/branding?

☐ Have you checked the idea for faults and limitations? What are they?

☐ Are there any problems the idea may create? What are the changes involved?

☐ How simple or complex will the idea's execution or implementation be? (In other words, will you need suppliers...are there any government regulations that may hinder the timeliness of introducing your products/services...do you need to import any products...do you have the right team in place to execute on your plans...? These are a few of the hundreds of questions you will need to ask yourself on implementation).

☐ Could you work out several variations of the idea? Could you offer alternative ideas? What will those additional ideas cost you?

☐ Does your idea have a natural sales appeal? Is the market ready for it? Can customers afford it? Will they buy it? Is there a timing factor? Is there a seasonal factor?

☐ What, if anything is your competition doing in this area? How will
    your company be competitive?

☐ Have you considered the possibility of user resistance or
    difficulties?

☐ Does your idea fill a real need, or does the need have to be
    created through promotional and advertising efforts?

☐ How soon could the idea be put into operation?

CHAPTER FOUR:
Looking at Different Businesses

Business Opportunities and the Legal Definition

When it comes to choosing a business, or even selling a business opportunity, you should be aware of some of the legal ramifications, as well as tax implications. I am not going to get into a lot of detail on these topics, I will leave the details to the attorneys and CPAs, but I do want you to be aware of the regulations that some states put on what they classify as a "business opportunity." Legal definitions of business opportunities vary, and not all states regulate business opportunities. The 25 that do regulate such opportunities are:

1. Arizona
2. California
3. Connecticut
4. Florida
5. Georgia
6. Illinois
7. Indiana
8. Iowa
9. Kentucky
10. Louisiana
11. Maine
12. Maryland
13. Michigan
14. Minnesota
15. Nebraska
16. New Hampshire

17. North Carolina

18. Ohio

19. Oklahoma

20. South Carolina

21. South Dakota

22. Texas

23. Utah

24. Virginia

25. Washington

Most Business Opportunity definitions contain the following:

- The person purchases goods or services that allow him or her to start a business.

- The purchase involves a certain amount of money. In 15 states and under FTC regulations, the minimum investment is $500; in the other 10 states the minimum investment is as little as $100.

- The seller makes any one or more of the following statements during the course of the sale:

  1. The seller will assist in securing locations for display racks or vending devices.

  2. The seller will return the money if the buyer is dissatisfied with the investment.

  3. The seller will buy back the products assembled or produced by the buyer.

  4. The seller guarantees (or, in some states, implies) that the buyer will be able to generate revenues in excess of the amount of the investment.

  5. The seller will provide a marketing plan or a sales plan for the buyer.

If a seller meets the definition of a business opportunity in states that regulate them, it generally means that he or she must register the offering with the state authorities and deliver a disclosure document to prospective buyers at least 10 days before the sale is made.

For more information on states' regulations, check with consumer protection agencies—often a part of the attorney general's office in your state.

With most business opportunities, you simply buy a set of equipment or materials and then you can operate the business any way you would like to, and under any name you want. There are no ongoing royalties in most cases, and usually no trademark rights are sold.

Since there is no long-term relationship, this alone can present a few problems and is primarily the business opportunity's chief disadvantage. Because there is no continuing relationship, the world of business opportunities does have its share of con artists who promise buyers instant success, then take their money and run. While increased regulation of business opportunities has lessened the likelihood of rip-offs dramatically, it is still important to investigate an opportunity thoroughly before you invest any money.

The Process of Buying or Selling a Business

While no two deals are ever the same, the purchase and sale of a business will typically fall into one of three categories:

- An asset purchase simply means that you're buying the assets of the business without necessarily buying the business entity itself.

- A stock purchase or acquisition means that you take over the business by stepping into the shoes of the existing owners.

- A merger refers to combining two or more existing businesses into one.

There are numerous pros and cons to each type of arrangement.

From a buyer's perspective, an asset purchase is sometimes the cleanest way to go. As a buyer, you could acquire all the assets of the business subject to an understanding that these assets would be free and clear of all liabilities. You also get what is called a "**step-up**" in tax basis for the business assets, which usually means you have more to depreciate. (Check with your CPA.)

In contrast, a buyer agreeing to a stock sale or acquisition can usually be held accountable for all debts and obligations of the corporation that's being sold. For this reason alone, many buyers decide not to go with just a stock sale.

On the other hand, a stock sale can be much easier to accomplish, because it may involve nothing more than swapping a check for stock certificates or ownership. The transition process is sometimes much easier with a stock sale, too, because title to the business assets remain with the corporation. The buyer is simply stepping into the shoes of the stockholder.

Depending on the size and complexity of the deal, there may be spin-offs, divestitures, or other undertakings that make it difficult to pigeonhole the transaction as an asset purchase, a stock purchase or a merger. However, most deals will progress in a similar manner:

1. Preliminary discussions

2. Negotiating a letter of intent

3. Signing a confidentiality agreement

4. Drafting and finalizing a formal agreement

5. Undertaking due diligence

6. Seeking approval from governmental authorities and consents from third parties

7. Possible management contracts as the business is transferred

8. Closing

9. Post-closing adjustments

Negotiating the Deal

Depending on the nature of the transaction, bringing a deal to closure could take anywhere from a couple of months to a year or more. Almost without a doubt, the process will take longer than you would have expected.

As early as possible in the process, an attorney and a financial advisor should be brought into the picture. One immediate benefit to doing so is that they may be able to help you structure the deal to your best advantage before the transaction takes on a life of its own.

Proper representation is critical even in **preliminary discussions**. Many unsuspecting sellers have signed something while in preliminary discussions—and later have regretted it. Obviously common sense dictates having a lawyer on your team before you sign anything.

Once the parties "shake hands" on a deal, the next step is usually to negotiate a **letter of intent**. The logic of having a letter of intent is to secure a level of commitment from the parties to show that they are serious about the deal. Otherwise, they may never get to the point of negotiating the finer points that always show up in the formal agreement. Unless you have some advantage to be gained from signing an enforceable letter of intent, it will usually be drafted as "non-binding" on its face.

As soon as possible, the other side is going to want access to the inner workings of your business to verify that it is everything you say it is. Before you turn over on your belly, though, you should have a **confidentiality agreement** in place to protect your interests—just in case the other side has unscrupulous motives. Believe me, these do exist in the world of business deals.

Somewhere along the line, a **formal agreement** will have to be finalized and signed. As deals evolve, the parties may not actually sign the final document until the deal is ready to close. There are almost always many drafts that go back and forth. This is where you absolutely need good legal representation, because the risks involved are just too great. If you feel you want to draft the agreement yourself, fine…but get a competent attorney to look it over and give a final stamp of approval.

The **due diligence** process involves "turning over all the rocks" of a business and looking to make sure that everything is in good order. Be ready to come under the microscope. Your business may be given more scrutiny than ever before.

Also keep in mind that the **government approval process** can be rigorous. One example is tax clearance certificates and certificates of good standing for your business entity. Sometimes, you may even need to get a governmental entity to approve a transaction before it goes forward. You will probably also need to get **consents from third parties** to assign contract rights.

The **closing** may involve a third party escrow company (especially when real property and public notices for "bulk sales" are involved). If there is an escrow, another level of documentation and compliance with the escrow company's requirements will be involved.

Some form of **post-closing adjustments** may be involved as well. One of the terms a buyer may negotiate, for example, is a representation that the business will perform at a given volume for a certain period of time after closing. Based on what happens, the purchase price may be adjusted up or down after the fact.

How's Your Insurance Coverage?

Like it or not, you need insurance. Don't run the risk of being caught without it. There are many types of insurance that you will need for your business and its key assets…people. I have come up with a short list of insurance types. This Insurance Worksheet will help you see what is needed and what your costs to have such insurance will be.

Take the time to fill out this worksheet and come up with the right mix of insurance for your business. Sit down with an insurance agent and go through this list. Although there are costs associated with getting the right amounts of insurance, they are far less than the costs associated with replacing what is lost.

EXAMPLES

The purpose of insurance is to transfer a risk that you can afford (i.e., the payment of a premium with no guarantee of its return) to cover a risk you cannot afford. For example, what homeowner does not insure their personal residence from damage due to fire?

Besides your attorney and accountant, another professional you will need to bring into the start-up process will be your insurance agent. It may be helpful to have one agent who can handle all of your insurance needs. There are policies available that are specifically designed to cover small businesses that, in one package, will cover most of your insurance needs.

Insurance is not only going to be important to you, but it will be important to your other business relationships. For example, if you choose to lease office space, the landlord will typically require that you furnish a certificate of insurance or be listed as an additional insured on your policy as assurance that your business will not disappear overnight in the event a loss occurs.

Here are some of the risks that should be protected by insurance:

Business Property Insurance

Property insurance should include a broad form of coverage to protect you from a wide variety of losses. Your insurance should include:

Buildings: Coverage would be required here if you own the building your business occupies. In the event you lease premises, your landlord should provide this coverage.

Business personal property includes your tables, desks, chairs and equipment. Also, you will want to include the tenant's improvements you might make to leased premises. An example would be a room divider you add, or a display case, or a custom built counter that forms part of reception area for your clients.

You will want to be sure that you are also insured against:

- Loss of Income

- Earthquake

- Flood (which may or may not be available)

Keep in mind that an all-risk policy can be structured to cover all of your equipment, including computer hardware and software, plus your valuable records. A properly written policy will include loss of income that might result from breakdowns, as well as loss of income from other hazards that would temporarily close down your business.

Liability Insurance

A Comprehensive General Liability (CGL) policy is designed to provide coverage to third parties for the following:

- Personal and Advertising Injury

- Fire Legal Liability, which is often mandatory if you lease your premises, protects you in the event your negligence results in damage or loss to your landlord's property. For example: You mistakenly leave a small electric space heater running and go home for the evening. During the night, the heater shorts and starts a fire, resulting in fire and smoke damage to your landlord's building. In this case, the negligent act of leaving the space heater on caused the loss. This is where Fire Legal Liability protects your investment.

- Products and Completed Operations

- Medical Expense or Medical Payments

- General Liability for your premises, the best illustration of which is the common "tripping over the torn carpet, resulting in an injury" loss.

On occasion, some policies will exclude Products and Completed Operations and/or Personal Injury and Advertising Coverage depending on the services your business provides. In these instances, a Professional Liability, Malpractice, or Errors and Omissions Policy might be available for your type of operation that will cover the errors and omissions that might result in suits against your company. This is particularly true of professions that are held to a higher degree of care or standard, for example, attorneys, engineering consultants, insurance agents, realtors, doctors and dentists.

Worker's Compensation Insurance

If your business has employees, Worker's Compensation insurance will be mandatory. Startup operations typically find that the State Compensation Fund can accommodate their needs. As the business grows, you can then "shop" for better prices for the coverage. In addition, some worker's compensation insurers provide additional services such as risk management and loss control services that may be beneficial to your business operation. These services are typically helpful in holding down claim costs over the long term. Do not confuse risk management with your taking part of the risk. The insurance company should assume 100% of the worker's compensation insurance risks.

Other Insurance

Auto coverage for company vehicles. (Liability, Comprehensive, Collision and Uninsured/Underinsured Motorists.)

Health insurance plans tailored to fit the size of your business. This coverage will help give you an edge when recruiting good employees.

Here's a type of insurance you might not think about: When you're not there—and when only your answers will do—it is good idea to have a guide prepared for your employees to know what-to-do, who-to-call and where-to-find-it information so as to maintain the momentum of your business.

Of course you should realize that you need to do a little pre-planning before jumping in with your checkbook and writing a check for all types of insurance premiums. **Before** you start-up, collect referrals to and references about lawyers, accountants and insurance agents so you can select the most appropriate professional advisors well before the time you will need their services. Perhaps they will provide you with initial free consultations for your considering them as members of your professional team.

Three large and reliable insurance companies that handle insurance for small businesses are State Farm, The Hartford and Allstate.

TOP TEN INSURANCE DO'S

1. Bring an insurance agent into your start-up process and have policies in place.

2. Consider using an insurance agent who can handle all of your insurance requirements.

3. Include excess liability "Commercial Umbrella" coverage for your business.

4. Use a broad form of business property insurance.

5. Consider a health insurance policy to recruit and keep good employees.

6. If you have employees, consider carrying employment practices liability coverage.

7. Maintain a clean and safe environment in your work place.

8. Include your tenant improvements in your property insurance policy.

9. Increase all your insurance coverage appropriately as your business grows.

10. Consider maintaining a buy-sell agreement with your partners, funded by life insurance, in the event of the death of a partner.

TOP 10 INSURANCE DON'TS

1. Do not consider self-insuring any part of your worker's compensation risk.

2. Don't fail to recognize regular employees as employees and not contract workers.

3. Don't overlook ongoing employee training on maintaining workplace safety.

4. Don't feel that you can't afford insurance. You can't afford not to have it.

5. Do not deal with contractors who cannot furnish insurance certificates.

6. Do not permit your insurance policies to lapse for non-payment of premiums.

7. Do not deal with insurance providers with substandard ratings.

8. Do not withhold information from your insurance provider. Provide them with a complete picture of your risks.

9. Do not go "uncovered" (uninsured) in any category of insurable and significant risk.

10. Don't overlook flood or earthquake insurance if in an area of high risk.

Use the Insurance Planning Worksheet on the following page to help you decide which types of insurance you should consider.

Business Insurance Planning Worksheet

Types of Insurance

Payment	Required (Yes/No)	Yearly Cost	Cost Per
General liability insurance			
Product liability insurance			
Errors and omissions insurance			
Malpractice liability insurance			
Automotive liability insurance			
Fire and theft insurance			
Business interruption insurance			
Overhead expense insurance			
Personal disability insurance			
Key person insurance			
Shareholders'/partners' insurance			
Credit extension insurance			
Term life insurance			
Health insurance			
Workers' compensation insurance			
Survivor-income life insurance			
Care, custody and control insurance			
Profit insurance			
Money and securities insurance			
Glass insurance			
Electronic equipment insurance			
Power interruption insurance			
Rain and flood insurance			
Temperature damage insurance			
Transportation insurance			
Fidelity bonds			
Surety bonds			
Title insurance			
Water damage insurance			
Total Annual Cost		$	$

Business Evaluation Checklist

If you are thinking about purchasing an existing business, take the time and answer some questions that will help you analyze what you are getting into. Evaluate your answers carefully and weigh the cost, the risks and the rewards of buying the business. This may take a little time, but it is well worth the time invested up front.

☐ Why does the current owner want to sell the business?

☐ Does the business have potential for future growth, or will sales decline?

☐ Is the business in sound financial condition? Have you seen audited, year-end financial statements for the business? Have you reviewed the most recent statements? Have you reviewed the tax returns for the past five years?

☐ If the business is in decline, can you save it and make it successful? If yes, why?

☐ Have you seen copies of all the company's contracts?

☐ Is the business now, or has it ever been under investigation by any government agency? If so, what is the status of the investigation? What were the results of any past investigation?

☐ Is the business currently involved in a lawsuit, or has it ever been involved in one? If so, what is the status or the result?

☐ Does the business have any debts or liens against it? If so, what are they for, and in what amounts?

☐ What percentage of the business's accounts are past due? How much does the business write off every year for bad debts?

☐ How many customers does the business serve on a regular basis?

☐ Who makes up the market for this business? Where are the customers located? (Do they all come from the neighboring community or are they from across the state, nation or world?)

☐ Does the amount of business vary from season to season?

☐ Does any single customer account for a large portion of the sales volume? If so, would the business be able to survive without this customer? (The larger your account base is, the more easily you will be able to survive the loss of a key customer. If, on the other hand, you only serve one large customer, the risk of losing that customer could put you out of business.)

☐ How does the business market its products and services? Does its competition use the same methods? If not, what methods does the competition use? How successful are they?

☐ Does the business have exclusive rights to market any particular products or services? If so, how has it obtained this exclusivity? Does it have a contract that clearly outlines its exclusivity? Can the business owner transfer this exclusivity?

☐ What intellectual property does the business own? Is the intellectual property in the name of the business or in the name of the owner? If it is in the name of the owner, will they sell the intellectual property with the sale of the business? Would the sale of the business include all patents, trademarks and copyrights?

☐ Are the business's supplies, merchandise and other materials available from several suppliers, or are there only a handful that can meets its needs? If you lost the business's current suppliers, what impact would that loss have on your business? Would you be able to find substitute suppliers in a timely manner?

☐ Are any of the business's products in danger of becoming obsolete or going out of style? Is this a "fad" business?

☐ What is the business's market share?

☐ What competition does the business face? How can the business compete successfully? Have the business's competitors changed recently? Have any of the competitors gone out of business? If so, why?

☐ Does the business have all the necessary equipment? If not, what additional equipment will it need and at what cost? Who will need to be trained, and at what cost? Will you need to add or update the equipment soon?

☐ What is the business's current inventory worth? Will you be able to use any of this inventory, or is it inconsistent with your intended product line?

☐ How many employees does the business have? What positions do they hold? How many will leave with a change of ownership?

☐ Does the business pay its employees high wages, or are the wages average, or low?

☐ Does the business experience high turnover? If so, why?

☐ What benefits does the business offer its employees?

☐ What insurance does the business carry, and is it transferable?

☐ How long have the top managers been with the company?

☐ Which employees are the most important to the success of the business?

☐ Do any of the business's employees belong to any unions?

What is a Franchise?

The Merriam-Webster Dictionary carries the following definition for a "franchise":

1. freedom or immunity from some burden or restriction vested in a person or group

2a: a special privilege granted to an individual or group; especially: the right to be and exercise the powers of a corporation b: a constitutional or statutory right or privilege; especially: the right to vote c (1): the right or license granted to an individual or group to market a company's goods or services in a particular territory; also: a business granted such a right or license (2): the territory involved in such a right

3a: the right of membership in a professional sports league b: a team and its operating organization having such membership

A franchise offers the freedom and immunity from having someone else make your decisions for you, as well as the freedom from the often-daunting task of building a new business from the ground up.

A popular saying in the franchise industry is, *"Be in business for yourself; not by yourself."* You'll more than likely see that repeated time and time again in the information you receive on various franchises available to you. Though perhaps overused, it simply and succinctly sums up the benefits of owning a franchise. All the pluses of owning your own business, without the imposing feeling of being alone as you build your enterprise.

Going into business for yourself is a great adventure, opening up whole new worlds of possibility and experiences to you. A new business owner is like an early explorer setting off to find new lands of opportunity...but even the best explorer needs maps and a compass to sail by and a clear destination.

To assist you further in your decision as to whether you should become a franchise owner, take a few minutes to fill in the *Franchise Evaluation Worksheet* before you go any further with your decision. The worksheet is broken down into five categories that are meant to provide you with additional information, sort of a *"snapshot view"* of the franchise opportunity you are looking at. The five categories are:

1. The Franchise Organization
2. The Product or Service
3. The Market
4. The Contract
5. Franchise Support

Rate your answers from one to four; four being the highest. Be honest with yourself. It's your time and money – not to mention your reputation—that will be at risk. If your score is higher than 100, the opportunity may be a good fit for you. If your score is under 100, take a closer look at the answers you gave and see where there can be some improvement. Some things may be out of your control if you would like to see changes occur. Focus on the areas that are in your control first, and then move to those that you might work with the franchisor to make a few changes. If your score is below 66, find another opportunity, and don't waste your time *and* your money. Good luck!

Franchise Evaluation Work Sheet

The Franchise Organization	1	2	3	4
Does the franchisor have a good track record?				
Do the principals of the franchise have expertise in the industry?				
Rate the franchisors financial condition.				
How thoroughly does the franchisor check its prospective franchisees?				
Rate the profitability of the franchisor and its franchisees.				
The Product or Service				
Is there demand for the product or service?				
Can the product or service be sold year round?				
Are industry sales strong?				
Rate the product or service in comparison with the competition.				
Is the product or service competitively priced?				
What is the potential for industry growth?				
Is the service or product easy to prepare?				
Is the service or product easy to understand and train on?				
The Market				
Are exclusive territories offered?				
How large is the territory?				
Rate the sales potential of the area you are considering.				
Is the competition strong in the area?				
How successful are franchises in close proximity to this area?				
Have any other franchises in the area had to sell, if so when/why?				
Are there expansion opportunities?				
Are you able to hold a first right of refusal on other territories?				
The Contract				
Are the fees and royalties reasonable?				
How attractive are the renewal, termination and other conditions?				
If the franchisor requires you to purchase proprietary inventory, how long before you turn the inventory over?				
If the franchisor requires you to meet annual sales quotas, are they reasonable?				
Rate how well you agree with any penalties associated with not meeting your quotas.				
Franchise Support				
Does the franchisor help you with site selection, lease negotiations and store layout?				
Does the franchisor provide ongoing training?				
Does the franchisor provide financing to qualified individuals?				
Are manuals, sales kits, accounting systems, personnel plans and purchasing guides supplied?				
Does the franchisor sponsor an advertising fund to which franchisees contribute?				
How strong are the franchisor's advertising and promotions programs?				
Does the franchisor have favorable national supplier contracts?				
Totals				

Self Test: Are you Compatible with Franchise Ownership?

The purpose of this test is to give you a good read on your suitability to own a franchise. Be upbeat when answering; avoid being hypercritical and preventing yourself from ever purchasing a franchise. Just be honest with yourself. You will really know if franchising is right for you.

1. Why specifically do you want to own a franchise? Is it to get rich, or is it to get on easy street and not have to work hard or work long hours? Is it to be your own boss and control your own destiny? Is it because you just can't stand what you're doing now? Explain

_____

_____

_____

2. Are you money motivated? Do you have to make more money? Do you feel that you are at a dead end where you are now?

_____

_____

_____

3. Do you fit in the corporate environment? Do you like working for someone? Have you ever been called a misfit, a maverick, or a malcontent?

_____

_____

_____

4. Do you really enjoy working hard, even if there is no immediate reward?

_____

_____

_____

5. How self-reliant are you? Do you wait for others to take the initiative? Do you need the approval of others and considerable support before you make a decision, start a task, or move in a new direction?

_____

_____

_____

6. Are you a risk taker? Are you willing to place your time, energy, and money into a venture that has the possibility of failing?

_____

_____

_____

7. Do you take real pleasure in being the boss, or having the authority and responsibility for the success or failure of a new venture?

_____

_____

_____

8. Are you a positive person? What makes you positive?

_____

_____

_____

9. Do you have good people skills? Can you interact with people effectively? Do you like people?

_____

_____

_____

10. Can you stick to the franchisor's system, or do you have to do everything your way?

_____

_____

_____

11. Do you like to teach? Do you enjoy training people in new tasks?

_____

_____

_____

12. Can you handle multi-tasking? Can you cope with the multiple demands of operating a business?

_____

_____

_____

13. Are you willing to accept the help of others?

_____

_____

_____

14. Do you have the determination to get what you want and go for it 100 percent?

_____

_____

_____

Think About Your Answers

1. This is an exceedingly important question. You probably will not get rich and you probably will have to work hard, long hours. Buying a franchise might not be a good move just because you can't stand what you are presently doing for a livelihood.

2. Being money motivated is important. This characteristic will tend to hold you in good stead when you have to work long and hard in the first two years of owning a franchise.

3. If you are very comfortable working for someone else, then owning your own franchise might not be for you.

4. In the first few years, operating a new business nearly always demands a hands-on approach which means long, hard hours and is definitely not easy street, at least not initially. Also, in the first two years, it's very common to not make a lot of money. You have to be able to wait on the reward.

5. You do have to be relatively self-reliant because you do have to manage the business day to day. However, one of the most significant benefits of owning a franchise is the support given by the franchisor. The phrase, "You are in the business for yourself but not by yourself," is very true.

6. Any way you cut it, you have to take a chance. There are failures in franchising. Yes, the failure rate is less than 10 percent, but the risk is still there. Can you handle it?

7. If you are the kind of person who enjoys being in charge, then having the authority and responsibility for the success of the venture will not be a problem.

8. Being a negative person is a luxury you can ill afford in business. Negative thinking begets failure. You simply have to be a positive person in order to succeed in business.

9. In nearly all franchises, good people skills are critical. If you don't have good people skills, you must be willing to develop them.

10. The primary reason that franchising is so successful is because the learning curve is transferred from the franchisor to the franchisee. The franchisor has developed a successful system. If you are going to be a franchisee, you must be willing to stick to the system. You have to do things the franchisor's way. Not your way.

11. The nature of franchising necessitates almost constant training for employees. It certainly makes it a great deal easier if you like to teach.

12. Operating a business requires wearing many hats. You have to be willing to do everything from mopping the floors to dealing with irate customers.

13. You simply must be willing to accept the help offered by the franchisor. It is valuable and it will help you succeed. Also, help is often forthcoming from employees. It's prudent to accept all help offered.

14. Achieving success does require a certain degree of inner strength. If you feel strong enough to make your franchise successful, then go for it.

Franchise and Business Opportunity Shows

National Franchise Exhibition	*Venture Marketing Group*	44-020-8394-5100 44-020-8785-3388
Franchise & Business Opportunity Show	*National Event Management*	800-891-4859 905-477-2677 info@nationalevent.com
Global Franchising & Licensing	*Singapore Exhibition Services*	65-02338628 Fax 65-8353040
National Franchise Show	*New Business Centre*	905-634-9750 Fax 905-681-1927
Be The Boss Expo	*Be The Boss Expo*	610-783-5060 Fax 610-783-1662
The Franchise Show	*Canadian Franchise Association*	

For additional information about these and future shows, contact the promoters:

mailto: shows@ausexhibit.com.au

MFV Expositions... (800) 433-4636 x815... 800-649-4433... (201) 226-1130... Fax (201) 226-1131... mfvinfo@mfvexpo.com

CHAPTER FIVE:
Different Business Structures

The Corporation

A corporation is the tried and true business entity through which investments are made, as a corporation could serve as a shield to help insulate investors from personal liability exposure. There may also be tax benefits to incorporating, even if the business fails.

A corporation is a legal entity that the law treats as a "person" in the sense that the corporation has its own name and identity separate from the owners. A corporation:

- Pays taxes

- Has the ability to contract

- Can own property

- Can sue and be sued

- Can sometimes be charged with and convicted of crimes

As a separate legal entity, a corporation serves as a shield between the owners and third parties doing business with the organization. So long as corporate formalities are observed, the corporate shield makes it difficult for third parties to go after the owners personally. Instead, creditors and other third parties can be limited to going after assets of the corporation.

The Sole Proprietorship

Although maybe not the best alternative in the long run, the simplest and cheapest way to start up a business is as a sole proprietorship. A sole proprietorship means that someone is doing business in an individual capacity and not through any type of business entity. You can invest in a sole proprietorship by loaning money to the business. However, if your investment is something more than a loan, the business may be deemed to be taking on another owner and would no longer be a sole proprietorship. Instead, there is a good chance that it would be labeled a partnership between you and the original owner.

The Partnership

A partnership involves two or more people undertaking a business venture as co-owners, with an intent to make a profit.

The General Partnership

Forming a general partnership is the easiest way to go into business with another person. Yet, the simplicity of a partnership can be its downfall, so careful planning is important. One of the principal drawbacks of a general partnership is that a general partner can be held responsible for all debts and liabilities of the partnership. For example, a general partner with only a 1 percent interest in a business could still be held liable for 100 percent of the debts and liabilities of the partnership.

The Limited Partnership

From a tax standpoint, it's sometimes better to invest in a partnership rather than a corporation. (Check with your CPA to determine whether this option would be best for you and your business). But, in order to address the issue of potentially unlimited personal liability, most states recognize another type of business entity that is called a "limited partnership." A limited partnership must have at least one general partner, but all of the other investors can be limited partners whose potential liability exposure can usually be limited to the extent of that partner's investment. One of the resulting tradeoffs, though, is that an investor must take a passive role in the operation of the business in order to maintain the status of a limited partner. In many regards, being a limited partner is comparable to being a shareholder in a corporation.

The Limited Liability Company

A limited liability company is perhaps best described as a hybrid of a corporation and a general partnership. It is treated as a corporation for limited liability purposes, but is treated as a general partnership for tax purposes. The owners are called "members." Unlike a shareholder or a limited partner, they don't have to take a passive role in the business. (A variation is the limited liability partnership, which can be formed in certain instances by professionals such as lawyers, accountants or engineers.)

The Nonprofit Corporation

Just because a business is called "nonprofit" doesn't mean that it can't make money. One significant limitation for nonprofit corporations, though, is that they cannot take on investors in the traditional sense, because they do not have shareholders. So the only way a person may be able to invest in a nonprofit would be through a loan or some other non-equity investment means.

Corporations (C-Corporations)

The label, "C-Corporation" merely refers to a standard, general-for-profit, state-formed corporation. Characteristics of the C-Corporation include the following:

Separate Legal and Tax Life

A corporation which is properly formed and operated as a corporation assumes a separate legal and tax life distinct from its shareholders. A corporation pays taxes at its own corporate income tax rates and files its own corporate tax forms each year.

Management and Control

Normally, a corporation's management and control is vested in its Board of Directors who are elected by the shareholders of the corporation. Directors generally make policy and major decisions regarding the corporation but do not individually represent the corporation in dealing with third persons. Thus, transactions with third persons and day-to-day activities are conducted through officers and employees of the corporation to whom authority is delegated by the directors of the corporation.

Shareholders

Shareholders are the owners of a corporation. Although shareholders have no power over the corporation's daily activities, shareholders possess the ultimate power in that they can appoint or remove directors of the corporation.

The Board of Directors is responsible for the long-term management and policy decisions of the corporation. While the directors are considered to have the highest level of DIRECT control over the corporation, there are, however, a few instances when the shareholders are required to approve actions of the Board of Directors (i.e., amendment to the Articles of Incorporation, sale of substantially all of the corporate assets, the merger or dissolution of the corporation, etc.).

Corporate Officers

Corporate officers are elected by the Board of Directors and are responsible for conducting the day-to-day operational activities of the corporation. Corporate officers usually consist of the following: President, Vice-President, Secretary, Treasurer.

Management and Staff

Management and staff are DIRECTLY responsible for the daily activities of the corporation.

One Person Required

In most states, one or more persons may form and operate a corporation. Some states, however, require that the number of persons required to manage a corporation be at least equal to the number of owners. For example, if there are two shareholders, there must also be a minimum of two directors.

Fringe Benefits

Corporations may often offer their employees unique fringe benefits. For example, owner-employees may often deduct health insurance premiums paid by the corporation from corporate income. In addition, corporate-defined benefit plans often afford better retirement options and benefits than those offered by non-corporate plans.

Corporate Formalities

To retain the corporate existence and, therefore, the benefits of limited liability and special tax treatment, those who run the corporation must observe corporate formalities. Thus, even a one-person corporation must wear different hats depending on the occasion. For example, one person may be responsible for being the sole shareholder, director, and officer of the corporation; however, depending on the action taken, that person must observe certain formalities: Annual meetings must be held, corporate minutes of the meetings must be taken, Officers must be appointed, and shares must be issued to shareholders. Most importantly, however, the corporation should issue stock to its shareholders and keep adequate capitalization on hand to cover any "foreseeable" business debts.

Shareholder Liability for Corporate Debts

Where corporate formalities are not observed, shareholders may be held personally liable for corporate debts. Thus, if a thinly capitalized corporation is created, funds are commingled with employees and officers, stock is never issued, meetings are never held, or other corporate formalities required by your state of incorporation are not followed, a court or the IRS may "pierce the corporate veil" and hold the shareholders personally liable for corporate debts.

Avoiding Double Taxation

Generally, the corporation is taxed for its own profits; then, any profits paid out in the form of dividends are taxed again to the recipient as dividend income and the individual shareholder's tax rate. However, most small corporations rarely pay dividends. Rather, owner-employees are paid salaries and fringe benefits that are deductible to the corporation. The result is that only the employee-owners end up paying any income taxes on this business income and double taxation rarely occurs.

S-Corporation Election

Another alternative is to elect the S-Corporation Status. Please consult an accountant or CPA. who knows and understands the intimate details of your business along with federal and local tax rules so that you can make the best decision regarding which form of business entity (S-Corporation or C-Corporation) will best suit your needs.

Duration of a Corporation

As a separate legal entity, a corporation is capable of continuing indefinitely. Its existence is not affected by death or incapacity of its shareholders, officers, or directors or by transfer of its shares from one person to another.

Constitutional Protections for Corporations

Although a corporation is not a "citizen" under the privileges and immunities clause of the Fourteenth Amendment to the U.S. Constitution, a corporation may exercise some of the constitutional protections granted to natural persons:

Right to Due Process and Equal Protection

Corporations enjoy the right to equal protection and due process of law under the Fourteenth and Fifth Amendments to the U.S. Constitution and under similar provisions of the California Constitution.

Freedom of Speech

Absent some narrowly drawn restrictions serving compelling state interests, corporations have the right to express themselves on matters of public importance whether or not those issues "materially affect" corporate business.

Right to Counsel

While a corporation cannot be imprisoned, a criminal action can result in fines and other penalties that could harm shareholders, officers, and other persons. Thus, a corporate criminal defendant has a Sixth Amendment Right to Counsel. Note, however, because a corporation faces no risk of incarceration, it has no right to appointed counsel if it cannot afford to retain private counsel.

No Privilege Against Self-Incrimination

Corporations have no privilege against self-incrimination (i.e., to prevent disclosure of incriminating corporate records.

The S-Corporation

An S-Corporation begins its existence the same way that a C-Corporation (discussed earlier) begins its existence—as a general, for-profit corporation upon filing the Articles of Incorporation at the state level.

However, after the corporation has been formed, it may elect "S-Corporation Status" by submitting IRS form 2553 to the Internal Revenue Service (in some cases a state filing is required as well).

Once this filing is complete, the corporation is taxed like a partnership or sole proprietorship rather than as a separate entity. Thus, the income is "passed-through" to the shareholders for purposes of computing tax liability. Therefore, a shareholder's individual tax returns will report the income or loss generated by an S-Corporation.

Qualifying for S-Corporation Status

To qualify as an S-Corporation, a corporation must timely file IRS Form 2553 with the IRS. This election must be made by March 15 of the current year if the corporation is a calendar-year taxpayer in order for the election to take effect for the current tax year.

However, a "new" corporation may make the filing at anytime during its tax year so long as the filing is made no later than 75 days after the corporation has began conducting business as a corporation, has acquired assets, or has issued stock to shareholders (whichever is earlier).

To qualify for S-Corporation Status, the corporation must:

> Be filed as a U.S. corporation (i.e., filed with any "state" office within the United States)

> Maintain only one class of stock

> Maintain a maximum of 75 shareholders

> Be comprised SOLELY of shareholders who are individuals, estates or certain qualified trusts, who consent in writing to the S-corporation election

> NOT have a shareholder who is a nonresident alien

<u>Losing S-Corporation Status.</u>

Failure to observe ANY of the above requirements could revoke S-Corporation status at any time. An S-Corporation that loses its status as such may not re-elect S-Corporation status for a minimum of five years.

Corporate Formalities

An S-Corporation follows the same state formalities as does a C-Corporation (i.e., filing Articles of Incorporation and paying state fees). However, an S-Corporation must make a special tax election under sub-chapter S of the IRS code, as described above.

IRS Filings

The S-Corporation must complete and file IRS Form 1120s to report its annual income to the IRS each year.

General Shareholder Requirements

ALL shareholders of the corporation must be U.S. Citizens or have U.S. Residency Status. If, for any reason, shares are somehow sold or transferred (even if by will, divorce, or other means) to a shareholder who is a foreign national, the corporation will lose its S-Corporation status and be treated as a C-Corporation.

Who Should Elect S-Corporation Status

Owners who want the limited liability of a corporation and the "pass-through" tax-treatment of a partnership will often make the S-Corporation election. In most cases, corporations that would benefit from S-Corporation status are those that plan on distributing the majority of earnings to its shareholders in the year those earnings are derived. Corporations who plan on retaining earnings for future investments in future tax years often choose the C-Corporation because under the S-Corporation, earnings will be taxed as if they were distributed to shareholders, regardless of whether a distribution actually occurred or whether the corporation retained the earnings for future investment.

Although I am happy to provide you with this information, I strongly urge you to speak with a licensed professional who can provide you with sound advice as to the form of entity that best suits your particular needs.

CHAPTER SIX:
Expanding Your Business

Analyzing the Market Environment

Conceptually, all of marketing is based on the idea that you must thoroughly know the environment in which your business operates in order to successfully promote and sell your product or service.

You may have developed a unique business idea, but why do you believe your idea will be successful? Is it based upon discussion of the idea or presentation of a prototype product or plan to friends and associates? If your business has been operating for a while, you've probably thought about branching out with new product lines, side businesses, or additional locations. How can you be sure the odds are in your favor as you pursue new directions?

Ultimately, your idea must fulfill a need for your buyers and must do so in a way that's somehow superior to the competition, however you define it. If you want to be sure that your idea will do these two crucial things, you need to know as much as you can about the following:

- Your competitors
- Your target buyers
- The marketing environment
- Market trends
- Future market growth

Your Competitors

The Information Age has increased the number of opportunities for new businesses and products and has tremendously increased the speed at which new products are developed and introduced into the marketplace. As a result, the Information Age has also increased the need for businesses to be thoroughly familiar with their competitors.

In order to compete effectively, you need to know:

- Who are your competitors?

- What are your competitors' strengths and weaknesses?

- What are your competitors planning to do next?

- What are your competitors' spending trends?

Buyer Identification and Behavior

Do you know who your buyers are? Do you understand why they buy your products or services? Assuming that other factors in making the product available (distribution) and known to the buyer (advertising and promotion) are in effect, influences on the buyer may be catalogued by:

- Culture

- Demographics

- Lifestyle

- Psychology of wants and needs

If your target buyer is also the end user of your products and services, then demographic, lifestyle, and other target buyer identification and classification are appropriate. However, if intermediate buyers are involved prior to products reaching the end user, other influences may be important.

For example, consumer packaged goods such as food, health, and beauty aids and household products may be initially purchased in large amounts by a master distributor, who sells to local/regional distributors. These local distributors often sell to a wholesale buyer representing a chain of stores. Finally, individual store managers decide to buy and stock the product before the consumer ever has a chance to buy the product.

Other buyer influences may be at work under these circumstances:

- **Profitability of the item:** The higher the margin and dollar profit per item versus competitive category products, the more likely the trade will accept it, regardless of product quality.

- **Discount deals available:** Discounts can increase margin, volume, and velocity of the item. For example, 10 percent to 25 percent off invoice each quarter for all purchases during the period are typical discounts for grocery and drug retailers.

- **Advertising and promotion support programs:** Multimedia TV, radio, print and public relations (PR) support, plus heavy consumer couponing, sweepstakes, and contests are typical consumer packaged goods programs that may be run one to four times a year.

- **Other cash deals:** For example, new item "slotting fees" are the subject of controversy and frustration for many manufacturers supplying grocery, drug, and mass merchandiser retailers. Slotting fees are cash payments and/or free goods that are not refundable, even if the products are dropped after six months by the retailer. Slotting fees range from a few hundred dollars to over $25,000 per item in some chains.

- **Free goods available:** For example, one case per store is common for new grocery item distribution.

- **Personal buyer/seller relationships**: There will always be personal relationships influencing buying decisions as long as there are people selling to people. That's why you hire good salespeople!

- **Sales incentive programs:** These programs may spur salespeople on to greater productivity and sales of a particular item or offering.

For example, grocery buyers of consumer packaged goods may have strict profit margin guidelines (i.e., minimum 25 percent on discount retail price programs), and minimum discount thresholds that they will accept (i.e., at least 10 percent off invoice). Buyers are also heavily influenced by brand advertising and promotion support programs (i.e., coupons in local newspapers on the promoted brand). For new products, cash payments to the stores for each new item (i.e., $500 to over $25,000 per item) and free case goods on each new item for each store are common for larger chains.

The more exact the identification of your target buyer, the more efficient your marketing programs will be in generating sales from regular or heavy users. For our purposes, let's divide target buyers into two groups:

- *End users who are the ultimate consumers or users of the product or service*—When appealing to the end user, you have to be able to put yourself in their shoes when it comes to purchasing a product or service. What psychological advantages can you offer them? What are they looking for, low price or high quality? What are the tangible benefits that they can relate to?

- *Channel buyers who are intermediary buyers between the company and the ultimate consumer/user* --What you have to look for here is quite simple: How will the channel buyer make money and are your prices low enough allow them and the retailer to make a profit? Of course, they will also look at the products you offer and consider whether they feel they can move your products at a decent price. Remember that 5 percent to 10 percent is a typical markup if you sell through a broker; a wholesaler will want to make 30 percent to 35 percent, and the retail store will want a 35 percent to 100 percent markup. Once you understand these markups, you will be better armed to establish your pricing.

The Marketing Environment

Today's marketing environment is influenced by the global marketplace and the explosion of the Information Age to a degree unprecedented in history. To be fully prepared, a company must recognize and understand:

- Cultural influences

- Governmental and political influences

- Demographic and lifestyle trends

- Local, national, and world economic trends

- The strengths of multi-national competitors

- The influence of technology on physical distribution

Local, state, and federal trade organizations are often the best source of information regarding the trends that are likely to influence your business.

Also, contact your local city, state, and federal organizations and agencies for more information:

- Chamber of Commerce, Rotary Club, local banks, etc.

- City planning commissions, regional county business redevelopment offices

- Minority-aid offices, state business development offices, state banking associations

- Federal regulatory and information agencies, such as the Small Business Association

- The Department of Commerce, and any agency that governs or buys from your type of business

The Government Printing Office (GPO) publishes many useful books to help you with research. If these publications are not in your local library, they can be obtained inexpensively from the GPO at your nearest Federal Building. Look in your white pages under the U.S. Government listings.

Examples include:

County Business Patterns—Put out annually by the Department of Commerce, with each state bound separately, these provide figures on employment, payrolls, number of businesses and number of employees in each business class.

County and City Data Book – This book by the Census Bureau gives you information on housing, population, income, health, retail and wholesale trade.

Future Market Growth

How big is your market? Is it large enough to sustain your business and competition? What is the growth trend for the next five years? Once a market has been identified, what is the size of the actual market that you can compete in? The actual market segment that you can sell to may be a small fraction of the total market. Each total market must be examined in light of:

- Size of the total market

- Size of the market that is interested in your products

- Size of the market that is available for distribution of your products

- Size of the market that already buys competitive products

- Size of the market that your company can serve

- Size of the market that your company can reach with advertising and distribution

For example, the *total potential market* for water purification and filtering devices is 100 percent of the world's population, almost five billion people, since everyone needs to drink pure water. However, the size of the *market interested* in water purification devices may be three billion people. The size of the *market available for distribution* may constitute two billion people. Yet, the size of the *market that currently buys* such products may be under 700 million people.

Assume your company is planning to introduce new water purification devices only in the United States and only in the outdoor/camping industry for portable water purification devices. Then the total *market you can serve* for your company's products may be only one million potential users, or 0.02 percent of the total potential world market.

What about the size of the market segment that your company can afford to reach with advertising and then distribution? Depending upon your company's resources and size, you may be able to effectively reach only 50 percent of the one million American camping enthusiasts through distributors who are willing to take on your product line. Assuming you are able to afford a modest print magazine ad campaign in two or three national industry magazines, perhaps 50 percent of consumers may be aware of your products, or a net 250,000 potentially interested, aware consumers.

If only one in four interested, aware, available, and servable consumers end up buying your product, you have potential sales of 62,500 units/year. Not bad, you say. But, if the repeat purchase rate is five years, you would need to generate an entirely new group of 62,500 qualified consumers each year, at least for the first five years. And this may be more difficult to execute than previously thought, with a total potential market of almost five billion souls! Perhaps you could increase the distribution base, increase advertising, or increase the served market to include other countries, or expand the product line by creating different sizes of portable water purification devices, or different units for varying severity of non-potable water conditions.

Primary Market Research

Primary research is concerned with the design and implementation of *original* research; that is, data collected from the source. The advantage of doing primary research is that you can get information on the specific question or problem you need answered, not information that merely applies to your industry or type of business in general.

Primary research is generally divided into two categories: "experimental" research and "non-experimental" research.

Experimental research. Experimental research is where the researcher controls and manipulates elements of the research environment to measure the impact of each variable. For example, a group of test subjects (who are consumers meeting certain criteria, such as frequent users of the particular product or service in question) is shown several television commercials, and, after each one, the group is asked questions designed to measure the likelihood that they'll purchase the product advertised.

Experimental research is often used by large consumer goods companies to test:

- the effectiveness of new advertising, or competitors' advertising
- the effect of various prices on sales of a product

- consumer acceptance of new products in trial and repeat-purchase levels

- the effect of different package designs on sales

Experimental research is further divided into two groups:

- laboratory studies, where virtually all variables are controlled except the one being tested, and testing is generally done on the premises of the research company

- field studies, where testing is done in the "real world," often by test marketing the product in a few locations to see whether consumers will buy it

As a practical matter, most small companies bypass expensive laboratory studies and utilize the real market environment to conduct field studies.

Non-experimental research. Non-experimental research is research done in the normal course of business, where the environment cannot be as closely controlled as in experimental research. Also the many variables of the "business" can't be as easily isolated. This research centers on measuring the entirety of a project rather than its separate parts.

Non-experimental research is divided into two categories:

- qualitative research, which seeks to obtain several subjective reactions from a limited number of test subjects

- quantitative research, which seeks to obtain the reactions of many test subjects to a limited number of questions

Non-experimental research is often used by companies to test:

- buyer responses to new products and product improvements (qualitative)

- buyer evaluation of advertising, packaging, and brand positioning (qualitative)

- effect of a 10 percent price increase on buyer purchase intent (quantitative)

- testing of a new formula against a similar competitive formula (quantitative)

Secondary Market Research

Secondary research is something every student has completed at one time or another, usually by doing library research with books and periodicals for a school report. This is usually the cheapest and easiest type of research for small businesses to conduct. However, it may be less reliable than primary research because the information you obtain was not developed with your particular problem or situation in mind.

Nevertheless, for some types of information (for example, questions about your competitor's market share, or the absolute numbers of potential customers for a new product), secondary market research is the only kind available.

Secondary research can be divided into two categories:

- external research, which involves looking at data gathered by industry experts, trade associations, or companies that specialize in gathering and compiling data about various industries

- internal research, which is data gathered by your company for purposes other than market research (i.e., sales reports broken down by product line) but which you can use to gauge what the market will do in the future

External Secondary Market Research

All businesses, large or small, need to know key information about their marketing environment, competitors, and target buyer/users. Smaller businesses may not be able to afford to purchase ACNielsen data for their industries at a cost of thousands of dollars per month. However, total market size, major competitors by category, and target buyer/user profile information is often available free from industry publications and trade associations.

The most commonly utilized external information includes:

- Trade association data

- Industry publications and databases

- Government databases (i.e., Census Bureau, state trade measurements)

- Sales, volume, and brand market share measurement systems

- ACNielsen Company — tracks retail store sales movement to consumers (yes, the same company that's famous for those TV ratings).

The American Marketing Association (the "other" AMA) may be able to help you as well. Write to them at 311 S. Wacker Drive, Suite 5800, Chicago, IL 60606, or call 1-800-262-1150.

Even for new businesses, internal company data from competitors may be available by interviewing competitor company executives, attending industry trade shows, and asking the right questions from industry "experts." They may be unaffordable as consultants but willing to direct you to free databases that you would not ordinarily know of or have access to. And don't overlook your competitor's suppliers. They can be excellent sources of information to aid your research.

For other free or low-cost external secondary research sources:

- Contact the editorial staff of trade publications.

- Search online search engines such as Google, Amazon, Yahoo or Alta Vista, etc.

- Contact local barter organizations and clubs like the Chamber of Commerce, Lions Club, and Rotary Club.

- Contact colleges and universities for departments/experts working on your field.

- Contact local, state, and federal government agencies.

- Contact international clubs and trade associations.

- Contact industry-specific advertising, promotion, and public relations agencies.

- Contact local and national broker, distributor, and private label manufacturers.

- Contact and interview buyer targets.

Internal Secondary Market Research

Secondary research involving the study of information generated by your own company is "internal" research. Here we're talking about information that was gathered for purposes other than marketing – for example, it may have been gathered for financial or management purposes. (If it was gathered for strictly marketing purposes, it would be considered primary research, not secondary.) The most commonly available internal company information includes:

- Daily, weekly, monthly, and annual sales reports, broken down by geographical area, by product line, or even by product

- Accounting information (i.e., spending and profitability)

- Competitive information gathered by the sales force

If you're in retailing or wholesaling, you have a wealth of information at your disposal if you keep detailed information about your sales, by product. You may be able to determine not only the types of products that sell best at various times of the year, but even the colors and sizes your customers prefer. There are a number of inventory tracking software products on the market that can help you keep track of all this information, not only for financial and tax purposes, but for marketing purposes as well.

Marketing Your Product

For most small businesses, highly effective marketing is a make-or-break necessity. It's really impossible for you to be successful without good marketing and sales techniques — that's what brings the dollars in the door. You've got to let people know about all the wonderful things your business can provide to them, which means that your business must first provide those wonderful things that people are willing to pay for. And that, in turn, means knowing who your customers are and getting so close to them that you can virtually anticipate their needs and desires.

This discussion that follows is intended to introduce you to some of the concepts and strategies that professional marketing experts in large companies use and show you how they can be adapted to help your small business thrive.

- The section titled, "Overview: The Marketing Challenge," presents a basic theory of marketing and introduces some key terminology.

- "Analyzing the Market Environment" discusses the competitive environment and cultural trends you need to examine in order to assess your business's place in the market.

- "Market Research" describes research techniques that you can adapt to fit your needs and budget.

- "Developing and Refining Your Product" emphasizes the importance of providing products or services that meet customers' needs, even before the first sale.

- "Packaging and Pricing Your Product" is a look at the impact of presentation and price on your product's success.

- "Choosing Distribution Methods" describes some of your options in getting your product or service to your customers.

- "Promotion, Advertising and PR" present the primary methods of communicating your message to your target customers.

- "Building a Successful Marketing Plan" shows you how to put it all together into a cohesive planning document that will become your blueprint to marketing success.

Overview: The Marketing Challenge

What does "marketing" really mean? To many business owners, marketing means two things: advertising and selling. However, I think that ultimately you'll be more successful if, every so often, you try to look at the "big picture" by taking the time to thoughtfully analyze your products or services and your business as a whole in relation to your competition, your customers, and to societal and regional trends and conditions.

You might say that the key to successful marketing is answering the following question for your business: *How will you communicate a meaningful difference about your business idea (product or service) to the people who might be most interested in buying it?*

There are a few important questions that should be answered for every business:

- What's unique about your business idea?

- Who is your target buyer?

- Who buys your product or service now, and who do you really want to sell to?

- Who are your competitors?

- As a small business, can you effectively compete in your chosen market?

- What positioning message do you want to communicate to your target buyers?

- How can you position your business or product to let people know they are special, in ways that are important to these buyers?

- What's your distribution strategy?

- How will you get your product or service in the hands of your customers?

Often your distribution method will provide an additional marketing channel or give you the opportunity to promote more products as you provide the first one.

Remember the Basics:

Quality — Do it better.

Promotion — Buyers must be aware of your product and motivated to purchase it.

Price — Do it cheaper or provide better value.

Distribution — Make it easy to get, to get fixed, or to get more of.

Market Research

Today, the world is defined by the term "Information Age." All businesses require accurate and timely information to be successful. Whether your company is large or small, the right amount of financing, equipment, materials, talent, and experience alone are not enough to succeed without a constant flow of the right business information.

Many large companies make market research into a very sophisticated and lengthy process, so that they can find out everything possible about their customers. For example, Philip Kotler, author and economist, writes in *Marketing Management*, "Coke knows that we put 3.2 ice cubes in a glass, see 69 of its commercials every year, and prefer cans to pop out of vending machines at a temperature of 35 degrees . . . We each spend $20 per year on flowers; Arkansas has the lowest consumption of peanut butter in the United States; 51 percent of all males put their left pants leg on first, whereas 65 percent of women start with the right leg; and . . .P&G once conducted a study to find out whether most of us fold or crumple our toilet paper. . ."

While you probably won't be able to afford a separate marketing research department to gather and monitor all the information that could possibly help you, all successful business owners must know their markets, competitors, customer wants and needs, and "what it takes to be competitive." It is not enough to know the answers to *what, where, when,* and *how* questions about your business. You also need to know *why* people buy your products and services. You should expect to budget at least a minimal amount of time and money for research, especially if you are starting a new business or branching out into a new direction.

Determine your market research needs and objectives. The first step in doing market research is to decide what you really need to find out. The kind of information you are seeking should determine the type of research you will do (although, of course, budgetary constraints will play a part in your decision).

Do you need to obtain a general feel for how key target buyers think about your product category and its various types of items, brands, and buying occasions? If so, interviewing groups of target buyers in focus groups may be the way to go, even though this type of research indicates only directional trends and may not be statistically reliable. Or is the confirmation of general trends in your industry sufficient? In that case, reading information from outside information services, industry trade associations, and industry experts may be all that you need to do.

You may wish to conduct blind tests of different formulas before finalizing recipes for a new product. In that case, you can do "laboratory" tests, where brands, packages, and names of products are not revealed to the test subjects, and achieve statistically reliable results at the 90 percent to 95 percent confidence level of predictability. Or perhaps you have completed extensive product development and testing and are now ready for a field test of your prototype products.

Market research procedures. Generally, market research procedures break down into the following categories:

- Primary research: Research involving the actual data-gathering about the specific usage patterns, product feature likes and dislikes, etc., of target buyers or current users of your products is considered primary research.

- Secondary research: Most of us are familiar with secondary research from doing library research with books and periodicals. With secondary research, someone else has done the actual data-gathering in the field and has written it up in a form that's easier for you to use. Secondary research is generally much less time-consuming and cheaper than primary research.

These two main types of research can be further broken down into sub-categories, as follows:

Market Research Data Collection

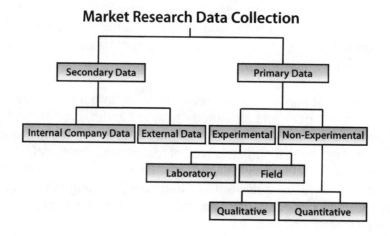

Market research possibilities for small companies. As you can see in the chart above, there are many market research techniques available. However, some may not be affordable or appropriate for your company. Managers of smaller companies may have to be more creative and proactive in:

- Deciding to do a limited amount of necessary research and setting affordable budgets

- Working with market research specialists or outside experts to define research problems and the design of the research

- Accepting the possibility of a greater number of errors or a "lower confidence level" in the mathematical predictability of research results due to:

  - Small budgets

  - Small sample sizes

  - Samples chosen in a manner that's not completely random

- Conducting and analyzing the necessary market research yourself or with company personnel

Developing and Refining Your Product

New businesses are always in a rush to get new products to market. Yet, how many new products or new businesses fail because the concept is never quite executed correctly for the intended target buyer? When a company doesn't take the time to do it right in the first place, it somehow always has to find the time to correct it later, often at great cost in unnecessary spending, lost time, lost sales, and lost market share.

The fastest way to go out of business is to introduce a great idea, but to never completely deliver the features or benefits that were promised. People who initially buy and then reject a new product are almost impossible to interest in trying the same *improved* brand again. Small companies who use the real marketplace to develop and refine a new product may never realize the sales potential of the product without a conscious plan for success.

It is estimated that over 40 percent of new packaged consumer products fail. Some 20 percent of new industrial products fail and 18 percent of new service products fail. If line extensions of current products are included, the failure rate for new packaged consumer products increases to 80 percent, according to Philip Kotler in *Marketing Management*.

A typical new product development path used in large companies (such as Procter & Gamble, Kraft/General Foods, Nabisco, etc.) can also be modified for new products by smaller companies:

- Company mission must be developed or confirmed.

- Product development strategy must be determined and refined.

- New product ideas must be generated.

- Ideas must be screened for potential profitability and fit with company goals.

- New product prototypes must be developed and refined.

- Packaging, pricing, and advertising strategies must be developed and refined.

- Success of the new product must be measured after introduction.

Packaging and Pricing Your Product

Packaging and pricing represent a very concrete way to communicate with your target market and express the positioning of your business.

- Package design is more than just the look of the product's physical wrapper or outer container that a product. Packaging can be the way in which services are bundled together for an intermediate buyer or end user. For physical products, the package label or wrapper may represent the product's entire business positioning, list of features and benefits, advertising, and promotion, especially for smaller businesses.

- Pricing must reflect not only your costs to produce the product or service at the expected volume, but also the value your customers place on what you offer. What's more, price is a way to differentiate your business from others, especially in the consumer market.

Choosing Distribution Methods

Once you have selected and developed a unique product or business idea, correctly positioned and targeted it to buyers, and developed your packaging and pricing, the selection of distribution channels and sales representation is key to successful marketing.

It's fairly easy to change many of your marketing tactics and strategies on a periodic basis. Pricing, packaging, and product mix are among these flexible choices. However, distribution and sales decisions, once made, are much more difficult to change. And distribution affects the selection and utilization of all other marketing tools.

There is a wide variety of possible distribution channels, including:

- **Retail outlets** owned by your company or by an independent merchant or chain
- **Wholesale outlets** of your own or those of independent distributors or brokers
- **Sales force** compensated by salary, commission, or both
- **Direct mail** via your own catalog or flyers
- **Telemarketing** on your own or through a contract firm
- **Cybermarketing**, surfing the newest frontier
- **TV and cable** direct marketing and home shopping channels

Distribution choices for a service business follow the same lines as those for a physical product. For example, financial planning services may be offered from printed material, sold at retail by consultants, delivered electronically by computer, or relayed by phone, fax or mail.

When selecting distribution and sales force representation, the following steps should be included:

1. Identify how competitors' products are sold.
2. Analyze strengths, weaknesses, opportunities, and threats for your business.
3. Examine costs of channels and sales force options.
4. Determine which distribution options match your overall marketing strategy.
5. Prioritize your distribution choices.

This exercise is applicable for both large and small businesses.

Promotion, Advertising, and PR

In order for your business to succeed, you generally need to promote your products or services to the same buyers that your competitors are targeting. Even if your business is one of a kind, you still need to tell target buyers that your business exists – with some kind of advertising or promotional communication. PR activities are another way to promote the image or reputation of your product. PR is similar to promotion and advertising, but can be more indirect, since some or all of the publicity a company's products and services receive from public relations activities may not be controlled by the company.

If you're a larger manufacturer of business-to-business goods, you may need to do much more personal sales promotion (to purchasing agents of your customer firms) than a consumer goods retailer, who would go to a promotion mix that emphasizes paid advertising.

- **Planning** promotional programs outlines the steps you need to take to create a comprehensive promotional game plan.

- **Promotion** ideas discuss a number of opportunities for materials or events that involve direct product purchase incentives.

- **Advertising** ideas discuss the use of advertising to inform, educate, persuade, and remind. This is accomplished with outside forces such as billboards, T.V., radio, and print ads in newspapers and magazines.

- **Public Relations** ideas discuss some indirect but highly effective ways of keeping your business in the public eye.

Let's focus on advertising first. To keep it simple, I would like to introduce a checklist for you to take a close look at as you develop your Advertising Strategy. This checklist is broken down into four areas of focus:

1. Overview

2. Specifics

3. Files

4. Competition

Take a few minutes and answer the questions posed in the checklist. This will get you thinking about your Advertising Strategy in a way that will save you a lot of time and, probably more importantly, a lot of money.

As a small business owner, you need to be vigilant about looking for ways to reduce costs and increase productivity and efficiency.

Advertising Checklist

Overview

☐ Have you defined your marketing goals and objectives and written them down?

☐ What exactly do you want to communicate to your potential customers?

☐ Are you communicating Buyer Benefits in your advertising?

☐ Have you strategized an advertising campaign? (What media will you use? What exactly is your marketing mix?)

☐ Is the timing right for an ad campaign? Why?

☐ Do you have a planned advertising budget?

☐ Can you meet the budget with the marketing mix you want to use in your campaign?

☐ Are you prepared for a successful response?

☐ Have you asked suppliers about cooperative programs?

☐ Have you made sure that employees (if any) are informed of your goals?

☐ Have all appropriate managers reviewed your advertising and approved of it?

☐ What is your lead time for ad placement?

Specifics

☐ Does your ad present a central idea or theme?

☐ Does your message require a response?

☐ Have you told customers where and how to find you?

☐ Is your ad clear and concise?

☐ Is your ad consistent with you desired business image?

☐ Has someone else besides you reviewed your ad?

☐ Do your ads match your branding (i.e., letterhead, Web site, company brochure, etc.)

Files

☐ Are you keeping files on all aspects of each ad?

☐ Where did the ad run? What were the results? (Number of sales? Sales increases?)

☐ How many potential buyers will see your ad(s) and what percentage response do you expect? What percentage do you think will be converted to buyers?

☐ How much did your ad cost, and what was your Return on Investment (ROI)?

Competitors and Customers

☐ Are you watching what your competitors are doing? (If advertisers repeat ads, try to determine why.)

☐ Where do your competitors advertise and how often?

☐ Are you willing to try something different, and is it worth the risk?

☐ Are you able to get ahead of your competition by having a story published about your business in the local newspaper?

☐ Do you conduct periodic surveys with your customers to find out what they like or dislike about your products and services?

☐ Are you listening to your customers? What do they want? What is important to them? What is not important to them?

☐ What media are most cost-effective to reach your customers?

Customer Satisfaction Survey Instructions

Customer satisfaction is another key to success. You want your customers to be happy with the products and services you provide. If they feel they have received good value for their money, your business will prosper. Getting your customers to tell you what's good about your business and where you need improvement helps you to be sure that your business measures up to their expectations.

A customer satisfaction survey is one way to gather this vital information. There are any number of ways to get such surveys to your customers. Copies can be included with orders, mailed directly at regular intervals, or sent and received by fax, whatever is convenient for your particular business. Many won't be returned, but those that are will make it worth your while.

The customer satisfaction survey below is designed to get your customers to tell you what they really think. No ranking of quality on a scale of one to five, no lengthy questions, just a list of key business activities and space to respond. Limiting the choices to "outstanding" and "needs improvement" sends a clear message that you expect the products and service you supply to be the best available, period. Keeping the survey to a single page—and printing it on company letterhead – makes it more likely that customers will take the time to respond. It also facilitates faxing. Be sure to include instructions on how to return the completed surveys. Give your fax number, include stamped, addressed envelopes, or whatever it takes to make it more likely that you'll get them back.

Don't forget to follow up on the comments you receive. If you have to change a procedure, tell an employee how you want things done, or pick a new delivery service, do it. Then advertise the fact that you did. Send thank you notes to the customers whose comments caused you to make a change. Let them know that you can do an even better job because they took the time to help you improve.

Sample Customer Satisfaction Survey

(Print on company letterhead)

As business owners, we are constantly looking for ways to improve the quality of our products and services. To do that, we need to know what our customers think. We'd really appreciate it if you would take just a few minutes to respond to the handful of questions below. As a valued customer, how you rate our work is the most important information we can get. Please help us do the job you deserve — the *best* possible!

Please return this survey [describe how you want the survey returned.]

Please circle "Outstanding" or "Needs Improvement" and comment:

Products: *Outstanding*   *Needs Improvement*
Comments:_____

_____

_____

Services and Support: *Outstanding*   *Needs Improvement*

_____

_____

Delivery: *Outstanding*   *Needs Improvement*

_____

_____

Ordering and Billing: *Outstanding*   *Needs Improvement*

_____

_____

Employees: *Outstanding*   *Needs Improvement*

_____

_____

CHAPTER SEVEN:
Building a Successful Marketing Plan

Every business, small or large, will be more successful with a business plan. And the key component the rest of the business plan revolves around, is the marketing plan. A good marketing plan summarizes the "who," "what," "where," "when," and "how much" questions of company marketing and sales activities for the planning year. Think of it in terms of the following:

- **Who** are our target buyers?

- **What** sources of uniqueness or positioning in the market do we have?

- **Where** will we implement our marketing spending plans?

- **When** will marketing spending plans occur?

- **How much** will we achieve in sales and profits; and how much will we spend?

The financial projections contained in your business plan are based on the assumptions contained in your marketing plan. It is the marketing plan that details when expenditures will be made, what level of sales will be achieved, and how and when advertising and promotional expenditures will be made.

Remember that a solid Marketing Plan consists of a few key components that make up the marketing design. First you will want to look at the primary components: Analysis and Strategy. As you *Analyze* the market you will want to uncover things like *Demographics* (who the people are); *Psychographics* (what makes them buy); *Market Size; Market Trends* and *Market Growth*. By analyzing these areas of your market it will help you to formulate a better strategy, and become more focused. The following items are really the primary elements of a marketing plan:

- The situation analysis describes the total marketing environment in which the company competes and the status of company products and distribution channels.

- The opportunity and issue analysis analyzes the major *external* opportunities and threats to the company and the *internal* strengths and weaknesses of the company, along with a discussion of key issues facing the company.

- The goals and objectives section outlines major company goals and the marketing and financial objectives.

- The marketing strategy section provides the company's marketing strategy statement, summarizing the key target buyer description, competitive market segments the company will compete in, the unique positioning of the company and its products compared to the competition, the reasons why it is unique or compelling to buyers, price strategy versus the competition, marketing spending strategy with advertising and promotion, and possible research and development (R&D) and market research expenditure strategies.

- The sales and marketing plan outlines each specific marketing event or action plan to increase sales. For example, it may contain a summary of quarterly promotion and advertising plans, with spending, timing, and share or shipment goals for each program.

Marketing Strategy

Every business owner should develop a written guideline that sets forth the business's marketing strategy. This document is used to judge the appropriateness of each action that the business takes. If a company has to take an action that is off-strategy, it may indicate a temporary emergency action prompted by competition or other factors beyond normal managerial control. Or it may indicate the need to change or revise the company's marketing strategy.

A good marketing strategy provides specific goals and should include:

- A description of the key target buyer/end user

- Competitive market segments the company will compete in

- Distribution channels

- The unique positioning of the company and its products versus the competition

- The reasons why it is unique or compelling to buyers

- Price strategy versus competition

- Marketing spending strategy with advertising and promotion

- Possible research and development

- Market research expenditure strategies

An overall company marketing strategy should also include:

- A definition of the business

- A description of the position of the business as a leader, challenger, follower, or niche player in the category

- A definition of the brand or business personality or image that is desired in the minds of buyers and end users

- An explanation of life cycle influences, if applicable

Use the following checklist to help create your own marketing strategy.

Marketing Strategy Checklist

☐ Define what your company is.

☐ Identify the products or services your company provides.

☐ Identify your target buyers/end users.

☐ Establish the marketing category (i.e., fast food purveyor, high-end audio equipment sales, etc.)

☐ Determine whether your company will be a market category leader, follower, challenger, or niche player.

☐ Describe the unique characteristics of your products or services that distinguish them from the competition.

☐ Define whether your pricing will be above, below, or at parity with your competitors and establish whether you will lead, follow, or ignore changes in competitors' pricing.

☐ Identify the distribution channels through which your products/services will be made available to the target market/end users.

☐ Describe how advertising and promotions will convey the unique characteristics of your products or services.

☐ Describe any research and development activities or market research plans that are unique to your business.

☐ Describe the image or personality of your company and its products or services.

Strategy statement tests. If the statements in your strategy are measurable and create action, as well as work to differentiate your company and products from the competition, congratulations! If they are not measurable, do not create action, and do not differentiate your company from the competition, revise them until they are.

A good working strategy does not necessarily need to be changed every year. It should not be revised until company objectives (financial, marketing, and overall company goals) have been achieved or the competitive situation has changed significantly (i.e., a new competitor comes into the category that is significantly different or new products emerge from existing competitors).

Sales and Marketing Plans

This section of the marketing plan outlines each marketing event or action planned to increase sales. The plan will generally cover a calendar year, broken down by month or by quarter. For example, it may contain a summary of quarterly promotion and advertising plans, with spending, timing, and share/shipment goals for each program.

Sales and marketing plans should be a logical outgrowth of short- and long-term company objectives and your marketing strategy. In the business plan, the sales and marketing plans provide an outline of each marketing event for the year, covering the following information:

- description of each event vehicle (i.e., media, promotion, trade, sales)

- timing of each event

- event goals and objectives (i.e., volume, share gains)

- cost of each event

- anticipated return on investment

Direct Marketing Do's and Don'ts

DO:

Keep your message simple. You only have a few seconds to get your prospect's attention—do it with a simple, powerful message that clearly tells what you are selling and what the benefits of your product are. Avoid too many details, especially on the cover of a brochure.

Determine your "Customer Profile." Examining your current customer base and determining its important characteristics is the starting point. You want to target the right audience for your product, so come up with a customer profile first.

Test. Many variables can affect the response to a mailing: the list, the offer, price and so forth. Test with smaller mailings—a few thousand pieces—to refine these variables before rolling out those big mailings. There is no mailer that consistently performs better than any others, so you have to test. This can help you avoid major mistakes.

Designing your mail piece. You want to include something that will make your customer react. A mailer that just tells them your businesses location and hours of operation won't get them to come running to your door. But a buy one get one free promotion just might!

- Personalization-the more personal you make your mailer, the better chance you will have increasing your response rates

- Giving your customer a time limitation helps as well (i.e., 25 percent off until the end of the month)

- Offering a free gift

Analyze the response. Make sure you can track leads and orders, so you can determine the return on your mailing investment.

Mail more than once. Repetition is important in marketing. After all, *repetition is the key to learning*. Mail at least six times a year to your prospects for maximum impact. In most cases, the effectiveness of your message will be enhanced by repetition. Be persistent, it will pay off!

DON'T:

Mail only once. Too many times, businesses use a mailing as a one-time "knee-jerk" reaction when things are slow. But this doesn't give a true picture of the potential. Like other kinds of advertising, repetition is the key to success in direct mail. You should mail at least six times to the same group to get best results.

Forget existing customers. Direct mail is a great way to stay in touch with your customers, offer them specials, and get more orders from them. You should mail to existing customers several times a year.

There are many good "how-to" books available about direct mail advertising. For further information, contact the Direct Marketing Association and ask for their "Publications Catalog."

Direct Marketing Association

Headquarters
1120 Avenue of the Americas
New York, NY 10036-6700
Telephone: 212.768.7277
Fax: 212.302.6714

Washington, D. C. Office
1111 19th Street, N.W.
Washington, D.C. 20036-3603
Telephone: 202.955.5030
Fax: 202.955.0085

www.the-dma.org

Example:

When I was a Sales Manager for an IT consulting company, we were a no-name company in a highly competitive market, and I needed to differentiate us from the competition. I had sent out a few letters to IT Managers, exhibited at trade shows, and even came up with a clever newsletter that was sent out every month…all to no avail. It wasn't until I figured out that my target market was buying other IT products from large, well known companies that things began to change The good news was that they were selling products, and I was selling a service. I was not in direct competition with them, and I had the brightest IT analysts in the valley working for me. Those were the people I needed to pitch my company to...the guys that had a great rapport with the same guys I was trying to sell to.

I began calling on every name-brand company I could think of—Novell, Microsoft, Cisco, Compaq, Peoplesoft, IBM, Dell you name it I called on them—to spread the good word of this new company in town that was a great value and had the brightest IT consulting staff to offer their clients on a temporary basis.

It worked, and worked big. We started doing joint marketing with direct mail pieces and doing seminars together; they also began taking us on appointments with them. And all of a sudden we were important, because "big brother" was looking out for us, and they were providing a solution for their clients--through us. This type of marketing is what I call Perception Marketing. When you give the perception that you are important, others take notice. It is not a cocky attitude; it is an attitude of confidence and assurance that what you have is pretty special. And, if you can get others to take notice, it can be a powerful closing tool.

We were able to sell about $8 million in consulting services in our region. I was then asked to share our success with over 350 managers in the organization. Once these types of methods were implemented and used in other parts of the country, another $60 million in revenue was generated.

We started to focus on niche marketing and started to take on projects that were on our clients' list of things to do, but just weren't getting done. I basically let them know that we were interested in showing them what we could do for them…and that we should take a look at the top 15 projects they had to complete in the next six months….we would handle the bottom three projects. This type of niche was something that we needed. Once the bigger players knew that we weren't primadonnas that only wanted to do the top projects, their walls of defense were dropped.

So that brings us to our discussion of *niche marketing.*

Have You Found Your Niche?

Niche Marketing is a concept that allows you to focus all of your collective energies in a very tight direction. It is a laser-focused attempt to carve out a specific area of customers. Instead of being broad-based, or "all things to all people," niche marketing allows you to focus your energy and your dollars in a refined, specific pattern.

Consider the example of Del Air, a company in Great Britain that literally manufacturers aromas for specific events and clientele. Del Air started out manufacturing air fresheners for home and autos, and then discovered a lucrative sideline…they created a niche of developing odd, nasty and even sundry smells, or aromas.

Apparently these peculiar smells are very popular as people want to re-create scents like the aroma of a Roman soldier's sweaty armpit after battle…or, capture the essence of a herd of cows in the Netherlands, standing in the meadows next to a field of tulips…or even to create the aroma of Frankincense. This type of niche is also very lucrative…one ounce of Frankincense costs $276!

The point is that air fresheners were nice, but odd smells were in big demand and the management team at Del Air figured out a way to deliver the fragrances at a premium price.

So how do you go about creating a niche that works for you and your clients? First, begin with answering a few questions that are meant to help you get a focus of where you currently are, where you want to be, and how to get there. The following list may help you:

Niche marketing has to be so tight that you must be highly disciplined to be successful at it.

☐ Who are your target clients?

☐ Who aren't your target clients?

☐ Do you refuse certain kinds of business if it falls outside your niche?

☐ What do clients think you stand for?

☐ Is your niche in a constant state of evolution?

☐ Does your niche offer what prospective customers want?

☐ Do you have a plan and delivery system that effectively conveys the need for your niche to the right market?

☐ Can you confidently predict the life cycle of your niche?

☐ How can your niche be expanded into a variety of products or services that act as profit centers?

☐ Do you have a sense of passion and focused energy with respect to your niche?

☐ Does your niche feel comfortable and natural?

☐ How will pursuing your niche contribute to achieving the goals you have set for your business?

Evaluating Your Niche

If you think you've identified a niche for yourself, you can use the following criteria to evaluate it and decide if you need to widen, narrow, or otherwise refine it.

1. Do you enjoy this particular type of work? Signs that you will enjoy your niche include:

- Looking forward to getting to work, especially on Mondays.

- Noticing that time seems to fly when you're working in your niche.

- Feeling satisfied after a day of hard work.

- Liking the clients and customers you work with.

- Feeling enthusiastic about letting others know about your work, even if you don't especially like marketing.

- Wanting to keep learning as much as possible about and get better at what you do.

- Preferring to do this type of work even if you could get paid more or have more clients doing something else.

2. Do you feel you're good at and well suited for this niche? Signs that you are include:

   - Your niche feels like an expression of the essence of who you are as a person.

   - The niche makes good use of your abilities and presents opportunities for you to grow.

   - Even if you know you still have much to learn, you feel capable most of the time while you're working.

   - Many aspects of your work come naturally to you, even if they're challenging at times, and you feel renewed from your work.

   - You like and enjoy the company of your colleagues in this field.

   - You like talking with others about the development of your work.

   - Your niche fits well with your desired lifestyle and your personal goals.

3. Is your niche narrow enough to clearly distinguish you from others? Signs that your niche isn't narrow enough include:

- Frequent comments by others that include: "Oh, I know lots of people who are doing that;" or, "That certainly is a popular field right now. You must have a lot of competition."

- Clients and customers frequently call to get price estimates so they can do comparison shopping.

- Frequent haggling over prices.

- Frequently losing business to a competitor.

- Having difficulty explaining how what you do is different from what others can offer.

4. Is your niche large enough to support you? Signs that you need to broaden your niche include:

   - You have difficulty finding enough clients and customers you can market to.

   - Clients and customers are happy with your work but can rarely make referrals or offer suggestions for how you could contact others with needs like theirs.

   - No matter how much or how effectively you market, you rarely have enough business.

   - The people who would most likely be able to put you in contact with your clients or customers tell you they rarely or only occasionally encounter someone needing what you offer.

5. Can you cost effectively and dependently reach people in the niche identified? Signs that you need to re-evaluate your marketing and advertising expenses in your niche include:

   - You are not able to use e-mail in your marketing efforts.

   - You have to spread your marketing message out many different print sources to reach your market (i.e., costly trade magazines, newspapers).

   - Direct mail is too expensive.

     – You have to purchase a mailing list that has far too many contacts to make if cost effective.

6. Does your niche have a future and can you foresee it evolving with emerging trends and changes in the economy?

     – Giant gumball machines had a fling for time, but did not have a sustainable long-term market…keep evolving your products and come up with ways to increase demand—at the same time increase the need for your new products.

     – Are there other products that will enhance your product line? What can you partner your products/services with to make them an even better deal?

     – If your product will need to keep up with technology, buying trends, and demands, then adapt the product and come out with new and improved items.

Action Steps: It's Time to Get Focused

1. Take an honest look at your business and evaluate whether or not you are sufficiently focused. Are you going in too many directions at once? Are you giving a 100 percent effort to what you most want to accomplish? Can you really juggle all those businesses at once?

2. If not, take this opportunity to review your original motives for wanting to be your own boss. Explore how you may have gotten sidetracked and why you haven't committed to one activity in which you can become well known, in demand, and sought after. Then, begin to narrow down what you can combine, eliminate or expound upon.

3. Ask colleagues, friends, clients, or customers to tell you what business they would say you are in. If they have difficulty being specific—or mention a variety of distinct activities, it's a sign you are not as focused as you believe you are. After the feedback, make adjustments and again ask them to define what it is that you do. This exercise can help you not only understand how others perceive what you do, but also to understand in what direction you need to move in order to get more focused.

4. Review your life's goals and priorities and think about what focus would be most compatible with what's most important to you in life. Remember to include your personal goals, your family goals, and your professional goals.

5. To help you decide on one business you want to become known for, weigh these options by asking yourself:

    a. Which things do I do best?

    b. Which activities do I enjoy most?

    c. What do I do that people need and appreciate most?

    d. In what areas do I have the greatest expertise and experience?

    e. What am I already best known for?

    f. What do I have the best contacts to do?

    g. What will people most readily pay me for?

    h. What involves the least risk?

    i. What fits best with my lifestyle and personal goals?

    j. What comes most naturally for me?

    k. What am I most eager to promote?

6. Make a commitment to your success by selecting a focus and begin now to devote your full efforts to that focus.

What Makes You Distinctive?

Before undertaking any further marketing efforts, it's vital that you take the time and energy to identify what you want to become know for. What do you want your customers/clients and our prospects to remember you for. What indelible qualities and traits do you want them to think about? Answer these questions before you undertake any additional marketing ideas or strategies.

1. What makes you distinctive?

2. What about you or your business stands out from the crowd?

3. Why do people choose you? Or, if you are just starting out, why *should* people choose you?

4. Who are you best suited to serve…and why?

5. What qualities, traits, skills, talents, etc., do you possess that you want your customers to know about?

6. What things are notable about you, your company, your products, etc., that will make you more memorable than anyone else?

7. What are the exemplary qualities that make you unique?

SIGNS THAT YOU'RE NOT FOCUSED

Although there can be other reasons you might encounter any of the following problems, each can be a sign that you are not being perceived as having a clear focus for your business. Check any that apply to you:

_____ 1. You have multiple business cards for your different business activities or wonder if you should.

_____ 2. You have purposely chosen a general business name that doesn't say what you do so you can use it for all the different things you do.

_____ 3. You often feel conflicted about which aspects of what you do you should mention when you introduce yourself.

_____ 4. People don't seem to take your business seriously.

_____ 5. People are often confused about or can't describe what you do.

_____ 6. Clients seem satisfied with your work, but rarely refer other business to you.

_____ 7. In trying to tell people what you do you often respond by saying, "I do a lot of things;" or you ask, "What do you need done?"

_____ 8. People have trouble explaining to others what you do or frequently comment that they never can keep up with all the things you're doing.

_____ 9. Your business cards and brochures include a list of things that other people are doing as fulltime businesses.

_____ 10. You have difficulty summarizing what you do in a simple sentence.

_____ 11. People seem to want to pay low, low prices for what you provide.

_____ 12. You are constantly looking for new businesses to start when you can't seem to make your current business work.

_____ 13. Your Web site is information-based only, and you do not drive the prospect to buy something from you or to at least contact you for more information.

_____ 14. You don't have a Web site.

Final Checklist for Your Web Site

Speaking about your Web site, take some time and write down your goals for what you would like to accomplish with a Web site. First, begin with your company's goals and objectives for the Web site. Then, develop the Web site from the bottom up, giving top priority to the intended audience/market and overall user experience.

Then integrate your current marketing plan and logo design into your site. This ensures your corporate identity is easily recognizable whether your client is surfing your Web site or reading your latest newsletter.

Strive to achieve Web standards and best Web site design practices, including those that will ensure quick downloads; easy navigation; and, most of all, consistency. Take a look at the following questions and find out where you stand...whether you already have a Web site or are just beginning your plans for developing one.

Web Site Checklist

	YES	NO
1. Have you developed your e-commerce strategy?		
2. Does your Web site include the five areas that make up a good site? (i.e., (1.) compelling content, (2.) graphics, (3.) commerce or the ability to purchase, (4.) quick load time, and (5.) a call to action.		
3. Does your site load quickly with a 56K modem connection?		
4. Do you have full contact information on your home page?		
5. Do you have a full contact information button/link on every page?		
6. Is your message clear?		
7. Is your site easy to navigate?		
8. Are there any dead ends that can be reached resulting in frustration for users?		
9. Are your graphics clean and eye-catching?		
10. Do your graphics load quickly?		
11. Does your site meet your original objectives?		
12. Do you offer additional data to your customers about topics of interest?		
13. Does your Web site mesh with the rest of your business?		
14. Are all of your products/services listed on your site?		
15. Have you submitted your site to at least 100 search engines?		
16. Is it easy to find your site?		
17. Have you put your Web site name on letterhead, business cards, and all print media?		
18. Do you offer your customers something worthwhile to come back to your site at a future time?		
19. Does your site offer a feeling of confidence and pride in your company?		
20. Does your site keep it simple?		
21. Is it easy to make payment on your site?		
22. Are you promoting your Web site in everything you do?		
23. Is the content fresh and up to date?		

CHAPTER EIGHT:
Recruiting and Hiring

Hiring an employee is truly making an investment in your business. When you hire someone to work for you, you will invest time, money, training, and trust. If you do it right, your business can move forward much faster than ever before; if you do it wrong, not only can you lose your investment, but you can be subject to lawsuits that can cause you to lose much more.

When most people think of hiring an employee, they tend to think only of classified ads and interviews. Yet, there's much more to successful hiring than that. It's an important process with serious implications for the future of your business, and you should put in the time to examine your needs and to hire and recruit in a systematic, legal way.

Some topics for consideration as you determine whom, if anyone, to hire are:

- **Should you hire someone?** Before you go about finding someone to work for you in any capacity, be certain that you'll need the extra help for the foreseeable future. You may be able to meet your needs without going to the time and expense of hiring an employee or other worker by working with independent contractors, temporary help, leased employees, or family members.

- **What legal responsibilities will you be exposed to?** Hiring the first employee is a big step — at a minimum you'll have to do payroll, withhold taxes, and supervise the person. In many cases you'll become subject to additional laws as you hire more people; for example, you may become subject to certain employment-related laws when you add a second, a fourth, or a fifteenth employee.

- **What do you need done?** Once you've figured out which staffing solution works best for you, take a look at exactly what tasks you want done. Using job descriptions can help here.

- **How do you let people know that you have a job opening?** Once you've determined what you need done and what type of worker you want, it's time to let the world know. Find out how to advertise and write job ads, and learn other ways of attracting applicants here.

- **How do you gather information from applicants?** After you've publicized the opening, you should have some applicants expressing interest.

- **Will you require that applicants complete applications, or will you accept resumes?** Have a plan on how to handle the responses and begin testing them, if necessary.

- **How do you interview candidates?** You've collected all the information, so now what? Work with your Human Resources professionals so that you know what to ask, what not to ask, and how to plan for your interview.

- **How do you check out an applicant's background?** In order to avoid negligent hiring claims and to protect your business, make sure that you thoroughly check references, credentials, and maybe even run a credit check.

- **How do you make the job offer?** After you've made your decision and chosen someone to hire, find out the best way to make a job offer.

- **What do you do after you've hired someone?** Once someone has accepted your offer, get all the necessary paperwork done quickly. Make the employee feel comfortable through orientation so that he or she can become a productive employee as soon as possible.

Should You Hire Someone?

When the work gets to be too much, you may find yourself toying with the idea of adding staff to help out. But do you really need help? First, ask yourself if you need to hire someone or just be better organized. If you're having trouble getting organized, try local libraries, community centers, or colleges for information or seminars on time management.

Can you afford an extra employee? Even if you know that you need the extra help, you'll still need to consider whether you can afford to hire a new employee. How do you know how much you can afford to pay? There's a tension between how much the employee's salary and benefits will drain your business's budget and how much extra money the employee's presence will bring in.

Look at your operating budget. How much slack is there in it? How much money could be cut from other areas, so you could use it to pay an extra person? Remember that you'll need to pay at least the minimum hourly wage, not only under federal law, but under your state's law. Don't forget about payroll taxes and legally mandated employee benefits, like workers' compensation.

Now, try to estimate how much extra income that employee would generate in the first year. This is not always easy to do. If the employee is going to sell your product or services, it will be easier to figure out how much extra income he or she would bring in than if the person is going to perform data entry or cashier duties.

In the absence of a "cause and effect" relationship, consider other ways that an employee could generate extra income:

- With an extra employee, would you have more time to market your services and expand your business?

- Would an extra employee allow you a chance to produce more products or serve more clients?

- Would an extra employee allow you to give your customers more efficient service or quicker delivery, with the result that higher quality would lead to more customers?

If the answer is "yes" to any of these, try to estimate how much extra business would be generated by more, faster, and better delivery of your product or service.

The math is simple. If you're fairly sure that the extra business would amount to more than the minimum salary of the employee, then you are in a good position to hire someone. If the added business does not outweigh the minimum salary that you would have to pay, then look for other alternatives to hiring a permanent employee.

Will you really save time? Once you've got someone to help out, you'll have all this extra time, right? Well, maybe. But don't forget, when you hire someone — especially when you hire for the first time — you have to invest a lot of time in the hiring process, in training the worker to get them up to speed, and in managing records.

If you're still sold on the idea of getting someone to take over some of your work, you'll need to determine your staffing options. There are several basic options to choose from and each has some pros and cons:

- Full-time employees
- Part-time employees
- Your children
- Temporary help
- Leased workers
- Independent contractors
- No-cost staffing methods

Employers' Legal Liability

If you decide to hire or lease employees or use independent contractors, it's extremely important that you become aware of all the federal and state laws that can affect your relationship.

Whether or not a business is subject to specific employment laws depends on how many employees that business has and for how long. There's a large array of federal and state laws and, in some states, it only takes one employee to make you subject to certain employment laws.

So, understanding your legal liability as an employer involves four things:

- Understanding the definition of an employee

- Knowing your liability under federal employment laws

- Knowing your liability under state employment laws

- Structuring contracts for non-employees to minimize liability

What if you're planning to use independent contractors only? Lots of business owners think that the way to get around all of the employment laws is to have no employees and, instead, to employ leased workers, temporary workers, or independent contractors. In some cases, this works, but how well it works depends on what the worker actually does and how you structure your contracts.

What Do You Need Done?

After deciding to hire someone, you need to determine exactly what you want the person to do for your business. Don't just think of it as "a little bit of everything" — try to narrow it down into specific tasks that you want taken off your hands. Before you start the process of hiring, figure out what you want — knowing what you want from your employee the best way to make sure that you get the right person for the right job.

Smart Tip:

Think of it this way: If you invest in an expensive piece of equipment for your business, you will probably compare prices. You will check with several vendors, compare features and prices, and then make a decision. When you buy clothes, you look for just the right fit. The same effort and care should go into making sure that you get just the right person for your job and that the fit is the best you can find.

There are three steps in the process to finding out what you need in an employee, and each can be as complicated or as simple as you want.

1. Do a job analysis to gather information and make decisions about the work to be done.

2. Determine the job qualifications for the position.

3. Create a job description to document what the job will entail.

How Do You Publicize a Job Opening?

Once you've determined that you need to hire someone and figured out what you need done, you're ready to let the world know about your job opening.

There are several ways to do so:

- Advertising. The most common means of advertising is in newspapers. Newspaper ads are relatively inexpensive and get good response and quick turnaround. Trade journals are more expensive and generate less response, but can be used effectively for highly paid, highly skilled professionals.

- Writing good job ads. There are some things you should include in your ads, and some things you should not include, particularly if you're covered by antidiscrimination laws.

- Personal recruiting. This involves going to places such as schools to find and attract job candidates. It can also include personal referrals.

- Outside services. If you tend to hire frequently or you need to hire several employees at once, this is a good route to use because they do a lot of the legwork. It can be expensive, though.

- Evaluating your choices. Remember that some situations might favor one method over another.

Screening Job Applicants

Once the word is out that you have a job opening, expect to get phone calls, in-person visits, and resumes in the mail. But what do you do once the calls, letters, and people start coming in?

1. First, determine whether the person is indeed an applicant. If you're hiring your first employee, chances are that anyone who expresses interest in any way is an applicant. If, however, you have 15 or more employees, the Equal Employment Opportunity Commission (EEOC) requires that you keep all records of all applicants for a full year, so determining who is an official applicant and who isn't becomes more important.

2. Decide how to respond to applicants. It's always a good practice to acknowledge everyone who applies for the job, even if you decide that they aren't suited for it.

3. Decide on the type of information that you are going to require from applicants and how you are going to get it. Do you have an application you want them to fill out or are you going to rely on resumes? Which other types of application materials could you ask for?

4. Determine if you're going to test your applicants. A few industries and jobs require certain testing, but most are at your discretion. What you need in an employee will determine what, if any, testing you want to do. Refer to the job description, if you have one, and see if any of the requirements necessitate testing.

How Do You Interview Applicants?

Once you've gathered the information you need from applicants and you've reviewed it, you're ready to start making some appointments to interview the most promising candidates.

Most people believe that they are good judges of character. Just a short chat with a job applicant and they can tell you whether he or she is hardworking, honest, creative, and loyal. Of course, it's usually not that easy.

Assessing applicants' qualifications by talking to them is a highly subjective method of choosing employees. However, used in partnership with other screening methods, such as applications and background checking, it can be an extremely useful selection tool. After all, one of the most important qualifications a person must have for any job is the right personality to work well with the supervisor and co-workers, and you can't get that information off a resume or application.

But, first you need to:

- Plan for the interview, by deciding where to have the interview and choosing an interview format.

- Know how to conduct the interview, by understanding your role as an interviewer, and knowing what to ask and what not to ask.

How Do You Do a Background Check?

After you've collected information about applicants and done several interviews, you're ready to check the background of your most promising candidates.

Because so many people misrepresent their background and credentials, it is important to do at least a little checking to see if what the applicant says about his or her background is true. A lot of employers don't do any checking, and they often regret that decision. The applicant may be unqualified for the job or may have some personality trait or past experience that causes problems for you later.

Moreover, if your applicant will have contact with other employees or with customers, an important reason to do that checking is to avoid negligent hiring claims. If you have an employee who turns violent and harms either a customer or another employee, you could be slapped with a lawsuit if reference checking would have kept you from hiring that person.

If you have employees who have or will have significant contact with the public, customers, patients, or children, you'll want to be particularly careful about doing a thorough background check, including a check of criminal records to the extent permitted by law.

For more information regarding how to do a proper background check, consider the following:

- General guidelines for reference checks

- Employment references

- Personal references

- Education records

- Credit reports

- Driving records

- Criminal records

- Documentation of the reference check

How Do You Make the Hire?

After you've interviewed your top candidates for a job and checked their backgrounds, you must decide which one you want to hire. Use the notes that you've taken in interviews to help you.

Now you're ready to make a job offer to your top candidate.

A job offer may be made first—either in person or over the phone—or in writing. I recommend you do it over the phone, so you get a quicker answer to the offer and so that your chosen applicant doesn't get snapped up by some other employer while your written offer is still in the mail. Then, put it in writing.

No matter what the form of the job offer is, the principle is the same. Do not make promises or statements that can be construed as promises, that you cannot or do not intend to keep. Those statements can sometimes lead to expensive litigation if you later decide to terminate the employee.

When a job offer is extended, it should include the following information:

- Position offered

- Location and working hours

- Salary (although sometimes salary must be negotiated before the applicant will accept)

- Benefits

- Starting date

- Any papers or information that should be brought on the first day of work

- A date by which the applicant must respond to your job offer, so you can move on to the next candidate if your first choice doesn't accept

While making a job offer is usually a positive experience, there are some areas to be mindful of and things to beware of. Don't create an employment contract with an offer.

What Do You Do After the Hire?

After you've made the job offer and the candidate accepts it, you can begin to take steps to:

- Complete the required paperwork (i.e., I-9, W-4, insurance application, credit card application, a copy of the employee handbook, etc.).

- Set up personnel files.

- Orient the employee.

- Review your recruiting and hiring process.

- Provide the proper training for their specific job responsibilities.

- Make them a feel a part of the team.

- Hold reviews after 30 days, 90 days, and six months. (These can be brief interviews to find out how happy they are…after all, it costs a lot of time and resources to hire them in the first place.)

CHAPTER NINE:
Business Planning 101

Overview

Normally, I would just refer you to my other books to discuss business planning—*Your First Business Plan, The Complete Book of Business Plans,* and *The Business Game Plan*—but for convenience, I cover the basics here. Without going into a lot of detail, business plans are used primarily for raising capital. However, there are other uses that a business plan can fill. They are each important in their own right, but serve a distinct function with a focus on a much different outcome. The primary four reasons to develop a business plan are:

- To raise money

- To gain a better focus

- To launch a new product or service

- To serve as a 90 Rolling Plan that plugs into a Strategic Plan
  I refer to a business plan that is never static, but is dynamic and always moving forward as a Rolling 90-Day Plan. Such a plan is always being updated as the business climate changes. In other words, it keeps changing by virtue of the fact that it is continually being updated.

- As a marketing tool to attract new strategic alliance partners

Whatever the purpose(s) of the plan, you will need to know about the basic structure of the business plan, and how to make it persuasive enough for others to take action. The basic outline for a good business plan should consist of the following elements taken from the Table of Contents of every business plan I write:

Executive Summary

Although the Executive Summary appears first in the plan, you should write it last. The reason for this is because it is a "summary" of the other sections of the plan. Wait until you're almost done so you can include the main highlights. You should cover the most important facts, such as product description, sales growth and profitability, management team, market analysis and strategic focus, and a financial summary.

The contents of the summary depend on the goals of your plan. For example, if you are selling a business idea to investors, then you should include highlights that will invite and encourage potential investors to read on. That might be growth rates, competitive edge, an exciting new technology, etc. On the other hand, if your plan is for internal purposes only, not to be read by outsiders, then your summary would probably not try to sell your plan, but just summarize it. Remember, as always, to match your plan to your purpose.

As a general rule, the first paragraph should include your business name, what it sells, where it is located, and the nature and purpose of the plan. You might also refer to the keys to success, or at least summarize them briefly.

Another paragraph should highlight important points. Projected sales and profits are normally included, and unit sales, and profitability. Include the news you don't want anyone to miss. That might be an important strategic focus for the plan, or new product or service, or media coverage, or something else.

In some businesses it might be taking on new partners, or new investment or expansion, or even cutting the expenses and preparing the business for hard times.

By default, this topic is followed by the highlights chart, which shows sales, gross margin, and profits for the next three years. Normally you should mention those numbers in the text.

Remember, this summary is the doorway to the rest of the plan. Get it right, or your target readers will not read on. Keep it short. (2-3 pages)

Company Summary

Use the Summary of the Company section to summarize the company-related information. Include details on the company's establishment, history, facilities and locations.

Although most business plans include a chapter describing the company, remember that *"form follows function."* For example, if your business plan is for internal use only, and all readers already know the company, you might delete this topic, which would also automatically delete all its subtopics. Describing the company may not even be necessary, and if it isn't, then don't spend the time. Modify your outline to suit your needs.

Take a paragraph or two here to introduce your business by explaining where it is, how long it's been around, what services it sells, and to whom, and who the owners or shareholders are. In the opening Summary of the Company, think of this as writing to people who will only read this summary, not the rest of the plan, and who don't want to know more than what you can put in a single paragraph.

Products and Services Description

This next section is about the services you sell, so in the sub-topics you will list and describe your products, present detail about how they are manufactured, where, at what cost, and by whom, and plans for future product development. This first topic can be a summary in three or four sentences.

The first topic should be the summary, so the next area provides more detail. List and describe the products your company manufactures or distributes. For each product, cover the main points including what the product is, technology, manufacturing cost, distribution, packaging, pricing, what sorts of customers make purchases, and why. What customer need does each product fill? What are the important features and benefits?

Include features and benefits of products, and remember that benefits are generally much more important than features, but people tend to describe features more than benefits. Benefits are what good marketers sell, but manufacturers tend to think in features first. Marketers' product descriptions tend to be rich in features, technologies, processes, and materials, but weak in customer benefits. With a high-speed modem, for example, most manufacturers would talk about the technology and the features, but what the customer gets is quicker response on the Internet, faster downloads, and perhaps other benefits like ease of use or ease of setup.

As you list and describe your products, you may run into one of the serendipitous benefits of good business planning, which is *generating new ideas*. Describe your product offerings in terms of customer types and customer needs, and you'll often discover new needs and new kinds of customers to cover. This is the way ideas are generated.

Market/Industry Analysis

Once again, the first paragraph is a simple summary. Assume that this paragraph might be included in a loan application or investment summary, so you need it to summarize the rest of the chapter. What information would be most important, if you had only one brief topic to include about your market?

Without going into great detail, you should generally describe the different groups of target customers included in your market analysis, and refer briefly to why you are selecting these as targets. You will also want to summarize market growth, and cite highlights of some growth projections, if you have this information available. Whenever you research and find data about your target market, make sure you source where you receive this information. Not only is it a good practice, but it provides credibility and validity to your business plan.

The depth of detail in the market analysis section will depend a lot on the type of plan. You may not need to provide a complete market study in a plan developed for internal use, when all of your team knows the market well. Maybe you'll just cite the type of customers you attract, and the part of town you serve. The market analysis section in a business plan is the area that is most likely to require research for information from outside your business, while most others require thinking and analysis of factors within your business.

Let's discuss the level of detail required. Remember that planning is about making good decisions, applying focus and enforcing priorities. A good useful business plan doesn't necessarily include a market analysis suitable for a Ph.D. candidate in market research.

If you are looking for an outside investment to fund growth, then you may have to use this section to display your wisdom and understanding of your industry, but don't overdo it. If you are planning in an internal plan and have no audience other than your own team, I recommend enough market research to make sure you're not missing key points. You be the judge.

Also, the value of information is limited by its impact of decisions. If more market information is not going to help you do something better, then don't bother to put it down in your plan.

In this section, you will also want to cover things like demographics (age, income, gender, occupation, education, etc.) or geographics (city, state, county, ZIP code, etc.), psychographics (what makes them decide to buy) and buying patterns (what has been established with trends and fashions).

Your analysis is based on a list of potential customer groups, each of which is a market segment. So, also explain how your segments are defined. The market segmentation concept is vital to your market assessment and market strategy. Divide the market into workable market segments—by age, income, product type, geography, buying patterns, customer needs, or other classification.

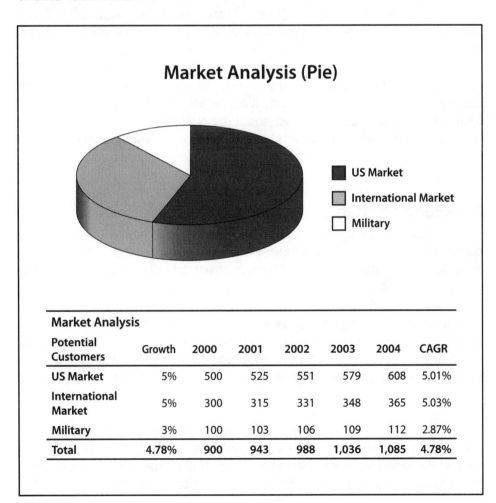

Market Analysis

Potential Customers	Growth	2000	2001	2002	2003	2004	CAGR
US Market	5%	500	525	551	579	608	5.01%
International Market	5%	300	315	331	348	365	5.03%
Military	3%	100	103	106	109	112	2.87%
Total	4.78%	900	943	988	1,036	1,085	4.78%

Companies selling to businesses would expect to divide the business into groups based on type of business, size of business, and geographies. Personal computer companies frequently divide their market into buying segments that include home, small office, large company, government, and education.

Be sure to include behavioral patterns and so-called psychographics, which produces the famous classification of "yuppies" as young urban professionals and, of course, the "Baby Boomers" with certain buying patterns. I've seen plans that focus on "high-end home office, technology-driven small business, and technology-phobic small business." Teenagers sort themselves into groups with names like "nerds, dopers, jocks, and greasers." Each of these labels actually stands for certain sets of behavior patterns and has some value in segmentation.

However you decide to segment your market, use this topic to explain the segmentation, define the different classifications, and develop as much information as you feel you need about the customers within each market segment group. Normally you would list for each segment the demographics, buying patterns, information patterns, and other important factors.

Marketing Strategy

In this section, you should introduce your marketing strategy. Sales strategy comes later. Your marketing strategy normally involves target market focus, emphasis on certain services or media, or ways to position your company and your service uniquely.

Your marketing strategy depends a great deal on which market segments you've chosen as target market groups. In this section as well, you will want to cover your Value Proposition, Unique Selling Advantage and Competitive Edge. Obviously, you want to make sure to preserve the same basic focus and themes.

The sub-topics of this section include the *positioning statement*, *pricing*, *promotion*, and whatever else you want to add. Target market focus is frequently added here, reinforcing the explanation from the earlier chapter. You might also want to look at media strategy, future business development, or other factors. Strategy is creative and hard to predict. Some of the sub-topics that follow this one will give you more ideas.

Create the information here as well that discusses promotion in a broader sense than simply sales promotion. Think of how you spread the word about your business to your future customers. Think of it in the broader context, including the whole range of advertising, public relations, events, direct mail, seminars, press releases and sales literature.

I know I have covered this previously, but repetition is the key to learning right? Think strategically. What, is your strategy about communicating with people?

- Do you look for expensive ads in mass media, or targeted marketing in specialized publications, or even more targeted, with direct mail?

- Do you have a way to leverage the news media or reviewers?

- Do you advertise more effectively through public relations events, trade shows, newspaper, or radio?

- What about telemarketing, the World Wide Web, or even multilevel marketing?

- Are you satisfied with how your marketing is working for you now, or is it a problem area that needs to be addressed?

- Are you meeting your needs and are they in line with your opportunities?

- How does your promotion strategy fit with the rest of your strategy?

- Check for alignment between what you say here and what you say in your value proposition.

- As you described market trends and target market segments, did you see ways to improve your promotion strategy?

When developing your strategy, remember that your competition is your opponent. Your game plan must be focused on how you will defeat your opponent and win the game. And, since you will be facing many opponents, your strategy must be broad-based, yet specific enough to hone in on the strengths and weaknesses of your opponents.

Management Team

Your management team can make or break your business. This team will sell your business concept better than the best financial projections, the greatest marketing plan, and even the most innovative product or service.

Make sure you cover the basic information first. That would include how many employees the company has, how many managers, and how many of the managers are founders. Is your team complete, or are there gaps still to be filled? Is your organizational structure sound, with job descriptions and logical responsibilities for all the key members?

Particularly with start-up companies, you may not have the complete team as you write the plan. In that case, be sure to point out the gaps and weaknesses, and how you intend to fill them. In addition, to make your management team better rounded, you may want to include your attorney, your accountant, your outside consultants, your insurance agent, and even an advisory board that is willing to assist you be a sounding board, or even help you make decisions as you grow your business.

You will also want to cover in as much detail as possible why your management team is qualified to drive your business to success. Discuss their experience and their areas of expertise as it relates to the business, and explain their functions within the company.

Internet Strategy

In the Internet Strategy section, explain what function the corporate Web site provides and what general information it provides about the company's products and services. Are customers able to order online at the present time through an e-commerce solution, or will that be coming down the road? Does the site still need to be upgraded with new options and menus for customers to receive real-time information and have the capabilities of viewing an online demonstration of the products offered?

Illustrate that the strategy is to develop a dynamic, robust site that may have real stream video capabilities to show how your solution works. It may even have a four- to five-minute overview of the products and services with a call to action. The call to action may provide the prospect or client with the opportunity to choose three options:

- Register to receive future information via the Internet.

- Sign up for a newsletter.

- Purchase a product online.

As you continue to develop strategic alliances with well known industry names, a further strategy may be to place a link from your site to the strategic partner's site, thus creating a portal of general health information for our customers and prospects.

In order to properly disseminate the information to the general public, the corporate Web site may need to be upgraded using the latest in Flash and video streaming technology. The initial programming can be outsourced to a competent Web design firm. This will save the expense of not having a fulltime Web developer on staff in the beginning.

Since there may eventually be a database developed that will be used for ongoing marketing and customer support, the programming will be required to be fully compatible with technology issues such as bandwidth, software, and support. This may cost a few thousand dollars to accomplish the e-commerce site you are planning.

Financial Plan

Provide the reader of the plan with summary of the Financial Section, and the followed it with detailed topics covering your general assumptions, break-even analysis, profit and loss, cash flow, balance sheet, and ratios.

As with all the Summary sections, you might want to write the topics first, then do the summary. How fast is the business expected to grow, and how do you intend to finance that growth? Or are you growing slowly and producing profits? What is your projected sales growth? Is this in line with the rest of the industry?

Another option is to summarize your financial plan in a more general way. This option fits when your financial plan is a significant piece of your expansion or your new business start-up, either because it involves new investment, or new loans, or a change in the way you do business with accounts receivable, or payables, or inventory. For example, if you are planning to grow your manufacturing business and finance growth by leasing equipment and factoring receivables, that might be an element of a new financial plan. A new long-term loan or major change in your short-term borrowing might also be part of a plan, even if these items don't show up clearly in charts and tables that you will create.

I suggest you create a table for the detailed topics listed above in the opening paragraph, as well as a chart that provides a graphical representation of the data in the table. For example, your Annual Sales Forecast table and corresponding chart could look like this:

Table: Sales Forecast

Sales Forecast

Sales	FY2004	FY2005	FY2006	FY2007	FY2008
Distributor Sales	$400,710	$601,065	$751,331	$939,164	$1,173,954
Retail Sales	$184,112	$736,449	$1,841,122	$4,602,805	$11,507,013
Home Shopping Networks	$357,294	$500,000	$875,000	$1,312,500	$1,968,750
International Sales	$48,600	$500,000	$1,200,000	$2,000,000	$3,500,000
Int'l. Bulk Consulting	$150,000	$300,000	$400,000	$600,000	$1,000,000
Total Sales	$1,140,716	$2,637,514	$5,067,453	$9,454,469	$19,149,717
Direct Cost of Sales	FY2004	FY2005	FY2006	FY2007	FY2008
Distributor Sales	$120,213	$180,319	$225,399	$281,749	$352,186
Retail Sales	$55,234	$220,935	$552,337	$1,380,842	$3,452,104
Home Shopping Networks	$140,381	$196,450	$343,788	$515,681	$773,522
International Sales	$29,160	$300,000	$720,000	$1,200,000	$2,100,000
Int'l. Bulk Consulting	$4,500	$9,000	$12,000	$18,000	$30,000
Subtotal Cost of Sales	$349,487	$906,704	$1,853,523	$3,396,272	$6,707,812

Sales Monthly

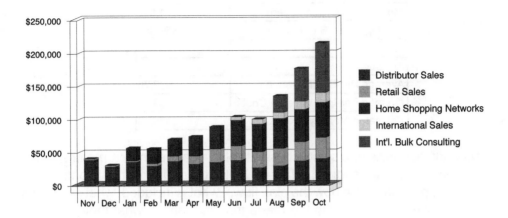

A Break-Even Analysis could be represented by a table and chart that would look something like the following table. Notice where the red, slanted line intersects the "$0" line on the left. This is your Break-Even Point.

Break-even Analysis

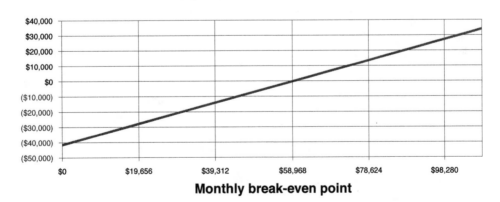

Monthly break-even point

Break-even point = where line intersects with 0

Table: Break-Even Analysis

Break-Even Analysis:	
Monthly Units Break-even	1,812
Monthly Sales Break-even	$59,359
Assumptions:	
Average Per-Unit Revenue	$32.76
Average Per-Unit Variable Cost	$9.83
Estimated Monthly Fixed Cost	$41,551

This workbook contains a sample business plan for a hypothetical manufacturing company. (See Appendix E.) Take a look at the different sections of the business plan and learn how the plan flows, what is included, what strategies are deployed and why, who the management team is, what their products are, etc.

CONCLUSION

This workbook was conceived from the many years of experience I have had in starting, operating, selling, succeeding, and "achieving results." I hope you have enjoyed reading and learning about a few elements of entrepreneurship, as much as I have living, researching and writing about it.

We have covered quite a bit of material up to this point. If you will take heed to the things that I have pointed out, you will be miles ahead of the game and will have a strong foundation as you build your business.

At the beginning of Chapter Two, I included a quote about dreaming, that I would like to remind you of here; **"If a man cannot dream he will soon be asleep to all the important things this life has to offer. If a man cannot pray he will soon only listen to himself. And if he has no charity for others he will soon be the only important thing in his pathetic existence."**

This is your time to dream and to achieve your dreams. You have all the tools around you to help you succeed. Take advantage of the materials that will help you learn how to best run your business. Don't get discouraged when you make mistakes, because you will. Learn from them and keep picking yourself up again, and again and again.

There is so much to learn…so don't get overwhelmed in the process. Take the time to learn from those who have been in the trenches, fighting the battles, learning along the way and achieving success.

Send me your success stories. E-mail me at bhazelgren@msn.com or bjhaze17@gmail.com to tell me about your successes and about the things you learn. Share with others some portions of your journey. Entrepreneurship is not a destination. It is an exhilarating adventure that offers many new learning experiences…most of the time on a daily basis. I wish you all the success and fun times in the world. Good luck in all of your endeavors!

Brian Hazelgren

APPENDICES

Appendix A.
Top 10 Goals Worksheet

Developing goals is always a good idea to help you get focused on what you are actually working toward. Goals are broad statements of ideal future considerations that are desired by you. In essence, they are statements of expectations or outcomes resulting from planned business and personal experiences. So, as you are thinking about what you want to accomplish, let your mind run wild. Don't try to harness the content…just write down what comes to mind. It will begin to take shape after you determine what you want, both in the here and now as well as the long-term.

Goal #1

Goal #2

Goal #3

Goal #4

Goal #5

Goal #6

Goal #7

Goal #8

Goal #9

Goal #10

Appendix B.
Nine Principles of a Highly Successful Business Plan

Nine Principles of a Highly Successful Business Plan—PART I

by Brian Hazelgren

I once overheard a conversation between two entrepreneurs that helped me draw a correlation and make an observation. One of them stated… "Writing a business plan is about as fun as getting a root canal!" The other entrepreneur said, "I've got one even better, it is about as fun as sitting down for a long conversation with my mother-in-law."

Sometimes I have to agree that it can create a little discomfort, but the process of writing a business plan can be highly rewarding if you follow a simple system and the proper outline.

You may have heard an investor or a banker make the statement: "I'm sorry, but before I make a decision, I will need to see your business plan." If you are looking for funding a business or an idea, a business plan today is as essential as a business card and an e-mail address.

Writing a business plan is time consuming and requires discipline. I have written over 130 business plans. I teach a course at the University of Utah on *Business Plan Development*, and I have written four books on this subject. In addition, I have read through hundreds of plans over the years. With all of this familiarity in business plan development, I am still thrilled to begin the process all over again and create a *magnum opus*, or work of art.

There are definitive pitfalls to look out for and some simple things to include in your plan to help you achieve your goals. I want to walk you through nine key principles that are basic steps in getting funding. When these principles are observed, I have seen millions of dollars raised for business ventures. Follow them carefully as you plan your venture and you will be far ahead of your competition.

Principle 1 – Convince yourself that proper business planning is an absolute necessity.

Your business plan is the heart and soul of your operation and is one of the most powerful tools you can provide to potential funding sources. It explains the four most important things they will look for in sizing up the opportunity… namely your Management Team, your Financials, your Marketing Plan and your Product or Service.

Your plan should outline the market potential and how your product or service will fit in to take a piece of the market. It communicates how well you have researched the opportunity, and lays out a *road map* from beginning to end…or at least for the next five years. It should also tell the potential sources of capital how you plan to capitalize on your strategy and create sales.

Next, your plan should clearly explain why your team is qualified to drive the business to success. In other words, surround yourself with a team that investors will be comfortable with. Finally, a good convincing of the potential of the business will exist with your Financial Projections. This is a key area of focus and will require forecasts for you to show to financiers.

Principle 2 – Understand why you need a business plan.

"Those who fail to plan, plan to fail." This old adage is not only profound and true; it is a simple process to follow. When you leave for a trip, you wouldn't just hop in the car, drive to the airport, book the first flight out that you see when you get to the counter, show up at a destination with no lodging plans, no car, no money and no sense of what you would like to do while you are there…wherever *there* may be; without a sense of how long you would like to stay, people you would like to meet, places you would like to visit, etc., and then still be able to enjoy your trip.

The same is true with planning your business. Have a plan. Commit your plan to writing. Put some serious thought behind it. Do your research. Come up with a compelling strategy that will make others want to participate with you…whether they are potential investors or key employees. Explain how you will compete in the market, and what your critical path to customer acquisition is.

If you don't have a plan, don't plan on getting any funding. It's that simple. Besides, you will be much better off by going through the process of developing a business plan. Two important things will occur in the process: 1.) You will better understand your business and will probably appreciate it more, and 2.) You will know if there really is an opportunity out there for you to snatch up your own piece of the American Dream.

Principle 3 – Take charge of your entrepreneurial life.

Think of it as a way for you to take control of your own destiny. A written business plan is evidence of your initiative. It shows that you have the discipline to focus your energies on an important project. Your plan will illustrate how you will achieve progress and growth, solve problems along the way, and accomplish your goals. Your business plan is the foundation of your vision and will allow you to structure your ideas into reality.

Principle 4 – Lay out a master blueprint.

A set of detailed architectural drawings is highly important to a builder...the same way a business plan is to an entrepreneur. Your plan will list the set of detailed procedures in building your business. It will also determine the details that will be used in reaching your objectives. Creating and reading from a set of blueprints in building a structure takes time and effort. Architects cannot neglect a single point of interest in developing the blueprints. If they do, the potential for disaster is certain.

Likewise, without a business plan the potential for disaster is very high. Your business plan is literally a master blueprint when you are developing a business. Blueprints for a building and a master blueprint for your business are very much alike. Isn't it interesting that a local municipality will not even allow the footings to be dug if a set of blueprints is not first approved? Funding sources view loaning money or investing capital the same way and take the position of, "Come and talk with me after you have your plan in writing."

Finally, each section of the blueprint is like a section of your business plan. Although they may be completely separate, they eventually must all tie together in the end to demonstrate a beautiful masterwork.

Principle 5 – Communicate your master plan to members of your team.

The business plan is a concrete statement of purpose that allows you to communicate to your associates and potential investment sources a step-by-step agenda for reaching your goals. Some portions of the business plan can also be used in training and coordinating meetings. You can even incorporate elements of your plan in explaining to your employees what their role is and how they will be accountable as you make the business function successfully.

The primary idea here is to have as many team members as possible involved in the process of crafting your business plan. After all, there may be several things they come up with that you probably never would have thought of. When your team is involved, they will be silently committing their energies to the success of the business. Involvement = Commitment, and Commitment = Success. This is a powerful way for you to find a greater degree of success, and keep your team enthused about the prospects of succeeding at all costs.

This concludes Part 1 of a two-part series on developing an investor-ready business plan. Part 2, below, further explains the principles that are critical in crafting a business plan that gets results.

Nine Principles of a Highly Successful Business Plan—PART II

In Part 1 of Nine Principles of a Highly Successful Business Plan, I discussed a recent conversation between two entrepreneurs and their viewpoint on writing a business plan. Their problem, like most people, was thinking more about the "pain" rather than the "gain." In crafting your business plan for your next project, focus on the REWARDS. Sure it will take a while to come up with a great plan, but think of the excitement and exhilaration of launching your business idea. Think of the freedom...the success...the journey, and the funding that you will receive.

Be creative in how to appeal to your audience. You don't need to be cutesy in loading your plan full of graphics on every page. Charts and tables are a definite plus as they provide a quick view of the numbers that you include in your plan. However, don't be consumed by showing fancy pictures or clip art on every page. That kind of artistic overload is a nuisance and doesn't impress investors. Be prudent regarding how you use graphics. Tables, financial charts, and pictures of your products are really all you need to make your plan stand out.

Become an artist for a little while and create that masterpiece. Create the type of plan that gets the results you are seeking. By the way, not all business plans are used for raising capital. Some are used to gain a better focus internally. Others are used to show a history of the business for selling it to a qualified buyer. Most of the business plans, as you know, are used for raising funds…from loans to private placements.

There are a lot of issues you will be faced with as you research, write, create spreadsheets, and compile your plan. If you feel you just don't know how to tackle all the issues in developing a solid business plan, then ask for help. This is a highly important step in the overall plans for your business. Don't skimp on details, and don't rely solely on your own abilities—however talented and experienced you may be. Get help with your research. Quote sources that are credible. Have your CPA review your numbers. Work with a professional who has loads of experience in writing business plans. But by all means keep control of the entire process. And, most importantly, have FUN.

Let's continue with the list of the nine key principles in developing a business plan that gets funded.

Principle 6 – The top four things funding sources will look at first are simple to recognize:

1) The Management Team. Very simply put, if your management team is not capable of driving the business to success, then the other three things won't matter. Make certain you have all the right players in management positions, or hire outside professionals to assist you.

2) The Financials. Provide past history if you have any; and projections for the future of the business as you see it, if funding becomes a reality. You will also need to provide information on how will you use the proceeds, and what you expect the new funding to do for your business. This area of discussion will focus on of a minimum of your Sales Forecast (including direct costs),

your Personnel Plan, your Profit and Loss Statement, a Pro Forma Balance Sheet and a Break-Even Analysis.

3) Your Marketing Plan. In this section, you will provide three important things: First, you must give a good overview of the industry: how large it is in terms of annual revenue, how many people make up the market you are penetrating, and the market growth and trends that have been established.

4) Your Product or Service. Provide a good overview of what your products and/or services actually are. Help the reader to clearly understand how your products/services are unique and why they will drive revenue. If you have multiple products or services, describe each one individually. Also provide any information on future products that will be forthcoming, either as a result of funding or from a natural evolution of the business.

Principle 7 – Know where to begin.

This may sound a little funny, but when it comes to writing a great business plan, a person can become completely overwhelmed trying to figure out where to start. After doing this for 21 years, I encourage you to take a few words of advice: Don't write your Executive Summary first (it is "summary" of all the sections of the plan); research your market/industry up front to see if your idea will actually be accepted; and try developing a few scenarios of a sales forecast—including direct costs, to see if the revenue will be there to support such an idea.

The rest of the plan will come together if you can identify that there is a need for your product or service and that you have the right team and all the right resources in place to make this idea become a successful reality.

Principle 8 – Develop a Solid Unique Selling Advantage (USA).

What makes your product or service unique? Why does it stand out from all the other products or services already in the market? Why will someone take their hard-earned money and give it to you first, over your competition? These are some very important questions that you will need to answer in a succinct way in order to convince the potential funding source to do business with you...not to mention convincing customers to buy from you.

Identify uniqueness by explaining what problems you solve. What benefits do you provide that no one else does? What qualities/traits/skills/talents., etc., do you possess that others don't? What things are notable about you, your company, your products, etc., that make you more memorable than anyone else? Take a few minutes and write down the answers to these questions. You will begin to see that even something as simple as staying open an extra hour, or having strategic locations for customers to visit you, is a great way to illustrate why you are unique and why customers will buy from you.

Principle 9 – Answer the most important question.

Every source of funding wants to know one thing. They are risking their capital in a venture that may succeed or fail. Therefore, when you are researching and eventually writing your plan, keep this question in your mind, because it will definitely be on the minds of your funding sources: "When will I get a return on my investment?" This is the silent question investors or lenders will ask after every section they read.

Sounds almost too simple, but make no mistake, if you can put a plan together that illustrates how you have thought this through in a thorough manner, you can raise the capital you need.

As you write your plan, try to answer this question as many times as possible. When you describe your goals and objectives, show how you are going to provide a good return on investment. As you explain your management team, illustrate how this team is highly qualified to look out for the bottom line. When you craft your marketing plan, explain by example how sales will occur as a result of your market analysis and marketing strategies. When you develop your financial projections, identify that you have clearly thought through the numbers presented.

However, since nothing is a sure thing, don't make promises that you can't keep. Don't over-forecast. Use the best conservative numbers that you can develop. Provide enough backup data from many sources that validate your idea or business concept. And, by all means, keep a careful watch on all the data written in your plan. Don't even allow partners to provide you with too much fluff. Validate every claim you make in your plan. Excitement for your idea is one thing, but deception is never a good strategy.

These last four principles of the nine overall principles are highly effective for raising the amount of capital you need to launch your idea, sell your business or fund your next venture. Do all this, and you will be granted a high approval rating. After all, the best flattery an investor can give is to part with their money and invest in your venture.

Appendix C.
Brainstorming Techniques

Brainstorming Techniques for New Ideas

By Brian Hazelgren

What is Brainstorming?

Brainstorming is an incredible tool that all executives should engage in with their team on a regular basis. In just a few short minutes a day, you can literally create new ideas that will move your company to the next level of success...or even start a new industry.

Brainstorming is the name given to a situation in which a group of people meets to generate new ideas around a specific area of interest. Using rules that remove inhibitions, people are able to think more freely and move into new areas of thought and, therefore, create numerous new ideas and solutions. The participants shout out ideas as they occur to them and then build on the ideas raised by others. All the ideas are noted down and are not criticized. Only when the brainstorming session is over are the ideas evaluated. This is the traditional way brainstorming is done. The aim of this article is to provide you with the methods of traditional brainstorming and then to move on to the next level and introduce a series of advanced techniques.

Some other definitions:

- Brainstorming is a process for generating new ideas.

- Brainstorming is a technique by which a group attempts to find a solution for a specific problem by amassing all the ideas spontaneously by its members.

- To brainstorm is to use a set of specific rules and techniques which encourage and spark off new ideas which would never have happened under normal circumstances.

- Brainstorming is a fun way to unlock all those exciting ideas that a group may have buried in their minds, but are too busy to think about.

- Brainstorming will help you come up with new ideas. Not only will you come up with new ideas, but you will do so with surprisingly little effort. Brainstorming makes the generation of new ideas easy and is a tried-and-tested process. Exactly to what you apply brainstorming techniques depends on what you want to achieve. You can apply them to develop new products, services and processes in your job, or you can apply them to develop your personal life.

You can think of this as either a holistic experience if you are naturally creative; or, if you are naturally logical, you can think of it as a process of following logical rules that will stimulate your mind to think of a problem from a different angle.

Naturally, there are techniques and environments that suit certain people better than others but brainstorming is flexible enough to be able to suit everyone. Whether you do brainstorming with a group of excited colleagues or you do advanced brainstorming by yourself in an isolated room will be up to your personal preference and circumstance. Both will be successful if you read and follow the process described here.

Tracking the history and use of brainstorming begins in 1941. Alex Osborn, an advertising executive, found that conventional business meetings were inhibiting the creation of new ideas and proposed some rules designed to help stimulate creative thinking. He was looking for rules that would give people the freedom of mind and action to generate and reveal new ideas. To "think up" was the original term he used to describe the process he developed and that, in turn, came to be known as "brainstorming." The rules he came up with are the following:

- No criticism of ideas.

- Go for large quantities of ideas.

- Build on each others ideas.

- Encourage wild and exaggerated ideas.

He found that, when these rules were followed, a lot more ideas were created; and that a greater quantity of original ideas gave rise to a greater quantity of useful ideas. Quantity produced quality.

Using these new rules, people's natural inhibitions were reduced, inhibitions which previously had prevented them from putting forward ideas which they felt might be considered "wrong" or "stupid." Osborn also found that generating "silly" ideas could spark very useful ideas because they changed the way people thought.

The Wildfire Spread of Brainstorming

Brainstorming has spread throughout the world. The technique is known to most educated managers; but, sadly, it is often applied ineffectually because of poor training and lack of access to quality training material. Nevertheless, it is used by nearly all of the world's largest companies and across a wide range of departments. Charities, government organizations and commercial companies all shout its praises.

Using the simple rules developed over 60 years ago, people are discovering new solutions to their problems and creating new opportunities to advance their companies and their own careers. It is one of the most exciting things ever to be the inventor of a world-changing product and to become the creator of the world you want to live in. Brainstorming promises you this and more.

Every single day there is a brainstorming session being conducted somewhere in the world. New ideas are flooding out of these sessions and society is changing because of it. Join in with the progress and make your ideas heard.

Rules of Brainstorming

Rule 1: Postpone and withhold your judgment of ideas.

Do not pass judgment on ideas until the completion of the brainstorming session. Do not suggest that an idea won't work or that it has negative side effects. All ideas are potentially good, so don't judge them until afterwards. At this stage, avoid discussing the ideas at all, as this will inevitably involve either criticizing or complimenting them.

Rule 2: Encourage wild and exaggerated ideas.

It is much easier to tame a wild idea than it is to think of an immediately valid one in the first place. During brainstorming, then, the "wilder" the idea, the better. Shout out bizarre and unworkable ideas to see what they spark off. No idea is too ridiculous. State any outlandish ideas. Exaggerate ideas to the extreme.

Use creative thinking techniques and tools to start your thinking from a fresh direction.

Rule 3: Quantity counts at this stage, not quality.

Go for quantity of ideas at this point; narrow down the list later. All activities should be geared toward extracting as many ideas as possible in a given period.

The more creative ideas a person or a group has to choose from, the better. If the number of ideas at the end of the session is very large, there is a greater chance of finding a really good idea.

Keep each idea short, do not describe it in detail—just capture its essence. Brief clarifications can be requested. Think fast, reflect later.

Rule 4: Build on the ideas put forward by others.

Build and expand on the ideas of others. Try and add extra thoughts to each idea. Use other people's ideas as inspiration for your own. Creative people are also good listeners. Combine several of the suggested ideas to explore new possibilities.

It's just as valuable to be able to adapt and improve other people's ideas as it is to generate the initial idea that sets off new trains of thought.

Rule 5: Every person and every idea has equal worth.

Every person has a valid viewpoint and a unique perspective on the situation and solution. In a brainstorming session you can always put forward ideas purely to spark off other people and not just as a final solution. Encourage everyone to participate, even if they feel they need to write their ideas on a piece of paper and pass them around. Encourage participation from everyone.

You will know that you have created a healthy brainstorming environment if everyone feels confident to contribute.

Appendix D.
Nine Signs of an Entrepreneur

Nine Signs of an Entrepreneur

It takes an entrepreneurial fire in your belly to start a business — and make it succeed — but not everyone has that fire.

How do you know if you have what it takes to start a business? There's really no way to know for sure. There are things in common among the emotional and family fabric of people ready to consider an entrepreneurial venture.

You don't have to fit all nine of these categories to be a good candidate for entrepreneurship. But it probably wouldn't hurt. In general, the more you have in common with these characteristics, the closer you most likely are to being ready to try going out on your own.

You come from a line of people who couldn't work for someone else. That is not meant in a negative way. People who are successful at establishing their own business tend to have had parents who worked for themselves. It's usually easier to get a job with a company than to start your own business; people who strike out on their own often have the direct example of a parent to look to.

1. You're a lousy employee. No need to sugarcoat this one. People who start their own businesses tend to have been fired from or quit more than one job. This is not to say that you were laid off for lack of work or transitioned from one job to a better-paying one — you were cut loose or you quit before they could fire you. Think of it as the marketplace telling you that the only person who can effectively motivate and manage you is yourself.

2. You see more than one definition of "job security." Many others are truly envious of the few people they know who've stayed with one employer for 25 or 30 years. They look incredibly secure. But, how many people do you know who are able to stay with one company for that long? In a rapidly changing economy, job security can be frighteningly fleeting.

Here's how one self-employed person puts it: "If I work for someone and my boss screws up, or decides he doesn't like me, or runs the company into the ground or any number of other things, then I'm out of a job. My security is tied to that one guy, that one company. But if a client decides they don't like me, or they go out of business or whatever, I've still got the security of all the other customers I have."

Or, to paraphrase one business observer (I think it was Dilbert), "It's way better to have 100 idiot clients than to have one idiot boss."

3. You've gone as far as you can go, or you're not going anywhere at all. Sometimes the motivation to start a new venture comes from having reached the top of the pile where you are, looking around, and saying, "What's next?" Early success can be wonderful, but early retirement can sometimes drive energetic and motivated people totally batty.

4. On the other hand, the drive to build something new can also come from deciding that you're stuck in the middle instead of at the top. Fear of stagnation can be a powerful motivator, especially if you have an idea for something that could be at least more interesting and potentially more lucrative.

Speaking of which . . .

5. You've done the market research already. Don't even talk about your great business idea if you haven't put the time into figuring out if there's a market for your product or service. As the people behind any number of failed ventures will tell you, "cool" doesn't necessarily translate into "profitable." Don't bother building it if you haven't figured out whether there's a good chance the customers will come. (For market research tips and online tools, check out Microsoft's bCentral's demographics section.)

6. You've got the support of your family. Starting a business is stressful under the best of circumstances. Trying to do it without the support of your spouse or other significant family members or friends would probably be unbearable.

7. You know you cannot do it alone. You might excel at promoting a business. Maybe you love running the financial end of the enterprise. You could be someone who starts a business because you have unique creative or technical know-how to create a product.

8. You know you will need to raise capital at some point. Let's face it, starting and operating a small business requires capital. Are you ready, or prepared to go out on a limb and mortgage your home, or ask others for money? Entrepreneurs know that this is inevitable. Even if you only need a small bank loan, an SBA guaranteed loan, or a line of credit…sooner or later you will need to be prepared to borrow money.

9. You have an unquenchable passion to win. Typically, entrepreneurs are competitive by nature and enjoy the thrill of victory. Even when you lose, you get back up again and again. Perseverance is a key element to your makeup, and quitting is not an option. You will find a way to succeed, or make something work to your liking – no matter what.

Any of the above is possible, but it's unlikely that you are going to excel at every one of these tasks — or at all of the tasks involved in running any business. Forget all that "lone wolf" stuff. No matter how "go-it-alone" your philosophy is, you're going to need some help sometime.

The willingness to get that help — having employees, partners or consultants for those areas in which you are not an expert — is one indicator of likely future success. As development consultant Ernesto Sirolli writes in *Ripples From The Zambezi*, **"No successful entrepreneur has ever succeeded alone. . . . The person who is most capable of enlisting the support of others is the most likely to succeed."**

Appendix E.
Sample Business Plan

Business Plan

FOR

ABC MANUFACTURING CO.

December 2004

Provided by:

Jim Allen
ABC Manufacturing

P.O. Box 1
Phoenix, AZ 85555
Telephone: (888) 555-5555
Fax: (480) 555-5555
www.abcmanufacturingcophxaz1.com

THIS IS A BUSINESS PLAN FOR REVIEW AND DOES NOT IMPLY
AN OFFERING OF SECURITIES

1.0 Executive Summary

The Company: ABC MANUFACTURING COMPANY is the original manufacturer of a multi-line of widgets. Originally developed in 1993, the widget was sold door to door as a gadget. Today the original design has expanded into a multi-line of products that range from super widgets to super gadgets.

The Company is in its second round of funding and wishes to raise capital in the amount of $500,000 for the following purposes: 1). For marketing costs, 2). For raw goods, 3). To establish a retail line for the products, 4). To expand the existing manufacturing facility, 5). To increase inventory, and 6). To hire key personnel.

ABC MANUFACTURING needs additional capital to fund growth and to roll out new products that have been developed. The past ten years have been successful building years for the Company. The products that have been developed are in high demand – with a 70%+ retention ratio. ABC MANUFACTURING is currently marketing and selling 14 product lines and is launching a nationwide television ad campaign in December 2003 that is anticipated to reach about 100 million households.

ABC Manufacturing, LLC has been in operation since 1993. The product was originally manufactured under the XYZ product name since 1982. Manufacturing was moved from South Dakota to the present Arizona facility. Today the Company has over 10,000 customers. During the past 24 months many positive things have happened that have spurred on new ideas in adding to the product line. New distributors from around the world have purchased larger than normal orders. The word is rapidly getting out that ABC MANUFACTURING products live up to the promises made by the Company. Developing a retail line of products was a highly necessary step in capturing additional market share.

The corporate strategic focus has been enhanced by these events and the Company is highly motivated to meet the demand. The recent market tests for retail giants such as Wal Big Stores, Simple Food Marts, Home Shopping Stores, Ohio Valley Marts and Super Giant Mega Stores have increased the brand identity for ABC. However the demand has also created the need for additional financing in order to meet demand.

The Market: The widget A market is estimated to be $6 billion at end user value in Q1 2003. This market is expected to grow at 4 percent annually according to professional forecasts published in Mediamedia Research. Well-known products accounted for the majority of the market penetration; however, they do not offer the same handmade widgets as do the ABC MANUFACTURING products.

Widgets B is used by over 25 million Americans, Widget C helps over 67 million Americans and Widget D is utilized by over 5 million athletes every year. The international market represents well over three times as many individuals that use the same widgets in the United States. The ABC MANUFACTURING products are marketed directly to these customers who require these types of products.

Marketing Strategy: Management has streamlined the Company to market and sell a multi-line of products through a combination of distributor sales, Web-based marketing and retail outlets. Specifically, sales are being generated through targeted e-mail campaigns, direct mail exclusive offerings and product displays located in retail stores, hardware sections of regional stores and at hospitals and doctors' offices. The Company will showcase four of its products in 210 markets nationwide through Triple ZZZ Shopping Network beginning in December 2003.

The foundation of the products is built upon the unique design of each product. The customer base is already in tact, the manufacturing lines are in production, the marketing strategy is accelerated, and with the ownership of the original design, ABC MANUFACTURING will be a streamlined business with a bright future.

Products and Services: There are variations of the main products in size and packaging, but the following represents ABC's tangible products line *1). Widget A, 2). Widget B, 3). Widget C, 4). Widget D, 5). Widget AA, 6). Widget BB, 7). Widget CC, and 8). A combination of all widgets.*

A list of the products with pricing and pictures is listed in Section Three as well as in the Appendix.

The intangible products of the Company consist of: Consulting contracts that are under negotiation with distributors around the world to set up manufacturing and labeling stations for distribution in certain countries.

Management: The management team brings with them many industry best practices and combined experience of over 100 years in manufacturing, banking, strategic planning, management, sales, general business management and Information Technology based applications. This is a solid team of professionals with experience.

Financial Status: The Company has been funded to date by Mr. Jim Allen and bank loans. Although this has been a necessary step to get the business off the ground for the first phases of operation, capital resources are needed to meet the demands of growth and expansion. With the additional funding, the Company hopes to reach $1 million in revenue for fiscal year 2004 and $25 million for fiscal 2008.

Use of Funds: The Company plans to borrow up to $400,000 to fund growth including manufacturing equipment, further develop its distributor network, purchase raw goods to meet the demand of new product introductions, expand its employee and distributor base, and provide marketing capital for the new products.

Financial Data and Exit Strategy: The Company intends to repay any loans in the time frame agreed to, or be acquired sometime after year five of this business plan. ABC MANUFACTURING may even opt to purchase back the shares of any outside shareholders if applicable. Any one of these options is intended to provide a remuneration event for the stakeholders and personnel who built the Company. Bank loans are intended to be paid off by year 2005, or sooner. In addition, the Company intends to be actively involved in mergers and acquisitions in year 2007 of this business plan. This will require additional capital if this is to occur.

Name and Company Logo: ABC Manufacturing™ stands for Always Being Careful, and it is an original, proprietary design used in all the widgets.

1.1 Goals and Objectives

1. Achieve a 10 percent response rate on direct mail and e-mail campaigns.

2. Convert 10 percent of the responses for the first six months after funding, and bump this number to 12 percent thereafter.

3. Operate a highly successful enterprise that continues to provide superior products.

4. Achieve the sales projections previously outlined.

5. Borrow $400,000 for the expansion of the enterprise and new products, as well as have commitments for capital for acquisitions.

6. Provide an exit strategy for any stakeholders after 2008.

7. Continue to develop new products that enhance the lifestyle of our customers.

8. Build a successful distributor channel with worldwide presence.

9. Achieve a Gross Profit Margin of 65 percent or greater.

10. Achieve projected milestones, as outlined in this business plan.

11. Have the products in 2,000 retail outlets by year five of this business plan.

12. Create jobs in rural areas close to the manufacturing and sales facilities. (Personnel Plan)

1.2 Mission and Vision

Mission Statement

ABC MANUFACTURING is dedicated to the manufacturing and distribution of superior products, as we provide the most effective products at a price that is affordable. We seek to create and nurture a healthy, creative, respectful, and fun working environment in which our employees are fairly compensated and encouraged to respect the customer and the quality of the product we produce. Our guiding principles are to exercise integrity in everything we do.

Vision Statement

ABC MANUFACTURING will always exercise integrity in its business dealings and strive to provide the finest products and services available for our customers. We will continually recognize our employees and customers as the lifeblood to the success of our operations and will treat each of them with respect and dignity. By so doing this will enable ABC MANUFACTURING to be a successful and profitable enterprise for our employees, customers and our financial stakeholders.

1.3 Keys to Success

The keys to success in this business are:

1. Uncompromising commitment to the quality of the products: quality components, efficient production, cost-effective packaging, and on-time delivery.

2. Successful niche marketing: locate the quality-conscious customer in the right channels, and we need to make sure that customer can easily find us.

3. A desire that all customers should have an enjoyable experience interacting with employees and technology of the Company when ordering products.

4. A high degree of product quality and consistency.

5. Management: Products and services delivered on time, costs controlled, marketing budgets managed. Remove the temptation to fix on growth at the expense of profits.

In today's market, individuals do not have the expertise to decipher what products are the best for themselves and their family. They simply want relief from the things that plague them. More often than not, consumers settle for the name of a product due to the marketing efforts of global conglomerates that saturate the airwaves with advertisements of grandeur. However, the products delivered generally have undesired side affects and may not provide the relief that the consumer is hoping for. Individuals are searching for products that provide relief but do not compromise on quality. ABC MANUFACTURING provides these products.

With eight mainstream products specifically geared to the challenge relief markets, ABC MANUFACTURING offers a wide variety of challenge relief solutions to individuals who suffer from discomfort and challenge.

Risks

Every business faces risks in today's economy and the products and consulting services ABC MANUFACTURING offers are no exception. There are three areas that are especially risky. The first is putting too much trust into one area of the business that is intended to drive revenue. If we do not have a solid mix of products and services, we may be vulnerable to market down turns and individual spending cuts.

The second area that represents a risk is allocating the right amount of capital to the development and marketing of all of the products. Management and investment sources must continue to provide the necessary capital to expand production and to expand into new markets.

The Company has balanced its revenue streams by offering a broad base of products and services. In the past, the Company has generated a majority of its revenues from the salve and material products. This heavy reliance on one product line is no longer the case. Management has taken this into account based on past experiences and has adjusted for sales variations, by basing its sales forecasts for expansion and growth with a balanced mix of products and services.

Contingency Plans

Management has developed contingency plans to mitigate the risks that were described in the last section. By providing a balanced mix of products, these risks should be reduced. Distributor channel, retail sales, and home shopping network sales are intended to make up a solid mixture of product offerings. Additionally, ABC MANUFACTURING will expand its sales efforts to increase the number of distributors in its core business to offset the time required to enter this market and generate revenue.

1.4 Use of Proceeds

Legal	$ 2,500
Marketing & Advertising*	$130,500
Travel	$ 48,000
Raw Goods	$ 75,000
Insurance	$ 10,400
Free Up Line of Credit	$ 40,000
Total Expansion Expenses	**$306,400**

Expansion Assets Needed	
Additional Inventory	$ 70,000
Other Short-Term Assets	$ 20,000
Total Short-Term Assets	**$ 90,000**
Long-Term Assets	$ 0
Total Assets	**$ 90,000**

Total Requirements:	**$396,400**

⟶

*Marketing & Advertising Mix	
Radio	$ 78,500
Literature	$ 4,500
Print Ads	$ 25,000
Direct Mail	$ 15,000
E-mail	$ 5,500
Web Design	$ 2,000
Total	**$130,500**

NOTE: These figures do not include landing a large national account.

2.0 Company Summary

The Company has experienced steady growth in customer acquisition and is currently expanding its sales internationally. The products are well received among contractors and homeowners. The Company continues to add new customers and distributors. With the expansion of international markets, the development of retail sales, and the product introduction to the television shopping networks, the Company is expected to grow at a more rapid pace.

2.1 Company Ownership

ABC MANUFACTURING, L.L.C., is an Arizona-based Limited Liability Company, currently owned by Jim Allen (75 percent) and Bob Smith (25 percent).

2.2 Company History

ABC MANUFACTURING was founded in 1993 by Jim Allen, and officially incorporated as a Limited Liability Company in June 1994. ABC MANUFACTURING licenses the original and highly guarded design of the products from Widget Company. Operating history for the product has been steady, except for fiscal year 2002, when sales dropped 13 percent due to a very sluggish economy. The following table and chart illustrate the Company's growth.

Table: Past Performance

Past Performance

	1998	1999	2000	2001	2002
Sales	$336,737	$408,034	$406,310	353,696	469,335
Gross Margin	$214,041	$279,253	$323,044	122,025	358,889
Gross Margin %	71.91%	68.44%	79.51%	34.05%	70.00%
Operating Expenses	$92,696	$128,781	$83,266	231,671	345,315
Inventory Turnover	12.00	12.00	12.00	6.00	12.00
Earnings	$56,776	$42,844	$48,887	55,949	(106,741)
Other Inputs	1999	2000	2001	2002	2003
Payment Days	30	30	45	15	30
Sales on Credit	$43,674	$40,803	$40,631	$35,050	51,350

Past Performance

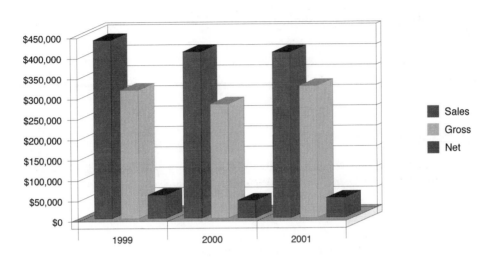

2.3 Company Locations and Facilities

ABC MANUFACTURING is located in Phoenix, AZ. The Company operates in a 7,500-square-foot building. The building is close to the Sky Harbor International Airport. The facility includes: office space, shipping area, stock area, ingredient mixing area and fill line area.

The manufacturing area has an automated manufacturing line; fluid steel mixer, including a cooling tunnel; and inventory equipment for shipping and receiving purposes. There are computer workstations running on an internal LAN system and a Meridian phone system for data and voice communication. ABC MANUFACTURING also has specialty software for shipping and financial accounting.

The fluid steel mixing area of the facility can accommodate a 16,000 gallon heated tank (800 degrees), which will be supplied by Steelco, USA.

The capacity of the line (per one eight-hour shift) is dependent upon product cooling capacity. Currently, ABC MANUFACTURING can fill 7,000 orders per day of its popular widgets. This equates to approximately 210,000 orders per month for one shift, operating seven days per week. The current fill line has the ability to run three shifts per day when necessary.

ABC MANUFACTURING also maintains a Sales and Marketing office in Mesa, AZ.

3.0 Products and Services

ABC MANUFACTURING offers superior quality widgets designed to effectively reduce costs...(continue summary)

3.1 Product and Service Description

Widget A

Reduces costs in every department...(write as much as you need to describe each product or service)

Widget B

Works with all types of mechanical devices...

Widget C

Keeps engines running smoothly...

Widget D

Speeds up the production process of copiers...

Widget AA

Increases cell phone range...

Widget BB™

Patented design to eliminate door squeaks...

Widget CC™

Increases the length of a long haul for semi trucks...

Widget DD™

A multipurpose widget used primarily for cleaning automobiles...

Consulting Services

ABC MANUFACTURING will continue to provide production consulting to distributors in other countries outside of the United States. This is a lucrative and steady market that exists for start-up and ongoing manufacturing and distribution consulting. With a mixture of consulting, strategic planning and production training, ABC MANUFACTURING plans to become a key partner with several distributors who rely on a strategic focus from the manufacturer to assist them in their manufacturing processes.

3.2 Competitive Comparison

Plans are to continue to differentiate ABC MANUFACTURING as a business partner with the vision of a company that wishes to be a strategic ally. Company products and consulting must continue to offer real value.

ABC MANUFACTURING benefits include many intangibles including superior products, vision, confidence, strategic direction, reliability, high-end product knowledge base, and the knowledge that someone will be there to answer questions and help at the important times.

Competing products to the ABC MANUFACTURING products are as follows:

- AAB209®
- Complete 2523®
- Breezee®
- W2X4J®
- KPLO22®
- 332211®
- Buttons3939®
- Star558899®
- Table3ONL®
- 91573XXJU®

These competing products are well known names in the industry. The power of marketing and advertising has created billions of dollars in sales for these products. At a glance, the following chart shows the ingredients of a few of the competing products. Note that none of the competing products has a special design.

ABC Manufacturing	Complete 2523	W2X4J	332211	Table3ONL
Dynamic Design	Static Design	Static Design	Static Design	Static Design
Titanium	Titanium	Steel	Brass	Nickel
Polished Aluminum	Aluminum	Copper	Tin	Tin
Gold Sprocket	Plastic Sprocket	Plastic Sprocket	Plastic Sprocket	Plastic Sprocket
Chrome Chain				

3.3 Sales Literature

ABC MANUFACTURING has developed sales literature that illustrates a highly professional organization with vision. Company literature also illustrates how the products enhance the way that other widgets work together. There will always be additional pieces of literature that need to be developed. To accomplish this, ABC MANUFACTURING is constantly refining its marketing mix through a number of different literature packets. These include:

- Direct mail with an introduction letter and product price sheet
- Corporate brochures
- Product information brochures
- Press releases
- New product information literature
- E-mail marketing campaigns
- Web site content
- Television advertisements

(Other copies of ABC MANUFACTURING advertisements and sales literature are attached in the Appendix at the end of this document.)

3.4 Sourcing

ABC MANUFACTURING manufacturers its own products, using mostly local and regional vendors of materials and services.

- Gold: Argentina
- Boxes / Plastic Containers: Colorado
- Containers / Jars: Utah
- Copper: Utah
- Steel: Arizona
- Labels: Utah
- Packing Material: Florida
- Shipping: UPS and USPS

The Cost of Goods Sold (COGS) usually runs the company about 30 percent. However, a more detailed cost per item is listed in the following table:

PRODUCT	SIZE	COST	WHOLESALE
Widget A	6 in dia.	$.91	$2.98
Widget B	8 in dia.	$4.22	$10.45
Widget C	10 in dia.	$19.44	$71.48
Widget D	12 in dia.	$29.41	$79.90
Widget AA	14 in dia.	$39.76	$81.59
Widget BB	16 in dia.	$49.30	$91.05
Widget CC	18 in dia.	$59.76	$101.59
Widget DD	24 in dia.	$71.60	$115.49

3.5 Technology

ABC MANUFACTURING Technology Management involves processes and activities that will establish standards and monitor the direction in all areas of our distributed computing environment. The further establishment of company standards and direction include operating systems, network LAN/WAN topologies, hardware, applications, and network protocols.

Technology is currently not as critical for the overall operation. However, as the Company continues to expand and grow, these areas will be of mission-critical importance.

4.0 Market Analysis Summary

The widget market is worth an estimated $6 billion at end-user value in 2003 and is projected to grow at 4 percent per year, according to professional forecasts published in Mediamedia, Inc., New York, NY.

Of the $6 billion, the United States' leading brands for challenge relief topical solution including AAB209®, W2X4J®, and Star558899® account for $4 billion of the market. The market is still large enough and fragmented enough to bear additional competition. Currently Star558899® and 91573XXJU® are heavily marketing their products via television and radio. Other such industry leaders include multi-level marketing (MLM) companies such as Sell a Lot, Next Sell A Lot and Keep it Coming.

*Source: Market research is from Mediamedia, Inc., New York, NY

4.1 Market Segmentation

ABC MANUFACTURING products cater to a variety of consumers that belong to several different market segments. Market research has shown the following market/industry classifications:

- Slow growth: 6.7 percent growth in the total market place with potential customers reaching over 25,000,000. Slow growth in the United States (figures from the National Slow Growth Foundation):

  - One-third of the entire population suffers from osteoarthritis.

  - 2.5 million Americans are afflicted with slow growth.

  - Juvenile slow growth affects 71,000.

  - Over one million Americans have been diagnosed with gout.

- Tendon Arthritis: 4.2 percent growth in the total marketplace, with potential customers exceeding 39,000,000.

- Back Strain: 3.3 percent growth in the total marketplace with potential customers exceeding 28,000,000.

- <u>Sports Injury</u>: 2.5 percent growth in the total marketplace with potential customers exceeding 5,000,000.

- <u>Diabetes</u>: 2.5 percent growth. Every year about 800,000 people learn they have diabetes. Over 25 million people in the United States, Canada and Mexico have diabetes.

- <u>Great Outdoors</u>: 2.0 percent growth. Kampgrounds of America (KOA) has over 500 campsites, and an estimated 8.5 million people go camping and hiking.

- <u>Volleyball</u>: 2.0 percent growth, with over 4 million volleyball players and over 3 million Badmitten players.

- <u>Lip Care</u>: 4.0 percent growth. There are over 200 million U.S. consumers of lip balm products

- <u>Lotions and Hand Cream</u>: 3.8 percent growth. There are over 175 million women in the United States, Canada and Mexico; and about 41 percent use lotions and hand cream.

*Sources: Mediamedia, Inc., New York, NY; Microharden; Cleaning Solutions of Ottowa

Market Analysis (Pie)

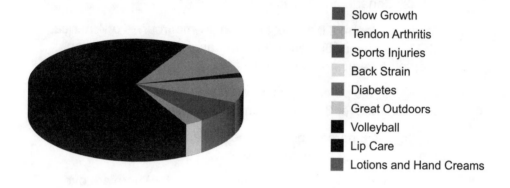

- Slow Growth
- Tendon Arthritis
- Sports Injuries
- Back Strain
- Diabetes
- Great Outdoors
- Volleyball
- Lip Care
- Lotions and Hand Creams

Table: Market Analysis

Market Analysis

Potential Customers	Growth	2003	2004	2005	2006	2007	CAGR
Slow Growth	6.7%	25,000,000	26,675,000	28,462,225	30,369,194	32,403,930	6.70%
Tendon Arthritis	4.2%	39,000,000	40,638,000	42,344,796	44,123,277	45,976,455	4.20%
Sports Injuries	2.5%	5,000,000	5,125,000	5,253,125	5,384,453	5,519,064	2.50%
Back Strain	3.3%	28,000,000	28,924,000	29,878,492	30,864,482	31,883,010	3.30%
Diabetes	2.5%	25,000,000	25,625,000	26,265,625	26,922,266	27,595,323	2.50%
Great Outdoors	2.0%	8,500,000	8,670,000	8,843,400	9,020,268	9,200,673	2.00%
Volleyball	2.0%	7,000,000	7,140,000	7,282,800	7,428,456	7,577,025	2.00%
Lip Care	4.0%	100,000,000	104,000,000	108,160,000	112,486,400	116,985,856	4.00%
Lotions and Hand Creams	3.8%	71,750,000	74,476,500	77,306,607	80,244,258	83,293,540	3.80%
Total	3.90%	309,250,000	321,273,500	333,797,070	346,843,054	360,434,876	3.90%

4.2 Target Market Segment Strategy

ABC MANUFACTURING is not advocating that it replace widgets intended for multiple uses, rather only for those who are demanding quality widgets that actually work. The ABC MANUFACTURING products are of higher quality, have higher amounts of ingredients, last longer, and are effective for a lower price than competitive national brands. ABC MANUFACTURING addresses the needs of the customer who has been unsuccessful in finding solutions using other well-known brands of challenge relief topical material.

Within the ABC MANUFACTURING market, there are many buyers who have tried several national brands without finding relief from their challenges. In ABC MANUFACTURING studies, 7 out of 10 people found that ABC's products relieve their challenges and will continue to purchase the product for many years, becoming very brand specific loyal. These people also become walking testimonials who share their positive attitude about the ABC MANUFACTURING products with others; they even share their purchases with other challenge sufferers.

4.2.1 Market Needs

ABC MANUFACTURING understands that the target market needs more than just a fancy marketing slogan or branding of a challenge reliever; consumers need a product that actually works. The target customer wants to have all of their challenge relieved so they can live their normal lifestyle to which they are accustomed. There is a need for superior quality—for *challenge relievers* without materials that can harm the body. As ABC MANUFACTURING customers mature, they become more knowledgeable about the materials within the products. When a customer has tried many of the other national brands without success, they begin to read labels and research what materials, when mixed together, will relieve their challenges.

ABC MANUFACTURING does not just sell challenge relief; it sells challenge relief with superior materials, and is backed by a 100-percent Money-Back Guarantee.

4.2.2 Market Trends

The ABC MANUFACTURING market has grown to recognize what works and what does not. The aging of the Baby Boomers is an important trend for ABC Manufacturing. The Baby Boomers seem to be educated on the products they use and in tune with the needs of their challenges. They understand and read labels to find solutions.

Athletes, medical professionals, and contractors are constantly looking for products that relieve challenges. The products developed by ABC MANUFACTURING cater to all ages of athletes, and particularly those that experience the need to be better at what they do. ABC MANUFACTURING serves a trend toward customers who desire additional products using the same materials. For this reason, ABC MANUFACTURING has formulated a widget with the highest blend of materials.

4.2.3 Market Growth

According to Mediamark Research, Inc., the market for Widget A is growing at a 6.7 percent rate; the market for Widget B is growing at a 4.2 percent rate; the market for Widget C is growing at a 3.3 percent rate; and the market for Widget D is growing at a 2.5 percent rate.

The market for Widget A should grow to 97,000,000 customers in the United States by 2010, which again is a projected growth rate of 2.5 percent to 6.7 percent.

The international market is about three times larger than the U.S. market.

*Market research is from Mediamedia, Inc.

4.3 Industry Analysis

The Widget A industry has undergone a great deal of change in the past decade. The introduction of new products found in the marketplace seems to be taking market share away from the dominant national brand such as 91573XXJU in the Widget A market; 332211 in the Widget B market; and Buttons3939 in the Widget C market. Star558899 produces relatively expensive widgets with fewer materials compared to the ABC MANUFACTURING products. Table3ONL and 91573XXJU are in the same price range, but do not contain as many challenge reducing materials.

Since ABC MANUFACTURING caters to several different markets as outlined the Market Analysis table, there are multiple areas of focus. The primary focus is to cater to markets that have a need for soothing challenge relief products. Each one of the markets that ABC MANUFACTURING sells to may have specific needs, yet the products fulfill those needs.

4.3.1 Distribution Patterns

The main volume in the industry is now concentrated in the national brands already mentioned, all of which compete for retail sales through all major retail chain stores.

Formulas are similar and quite competitive, costs and cost control is critical, channel management and channel marketing is the key to these corporations' continued success.

There are also some smaller manufacturers still making deep challenge relief products for small niche markets such as, challenge A, challenge B, challenge C, etc. Most of these are small companies, with one member in their product family.

4.3.2 Competition and Buying Patterns

The primary manufacturers are selling directly to the chain stores and hardware distribution markets. This accounts for their main volume of distribution. The challenge relief customer seems to be growing more comfortable with purchasing new or improved products that might relieve their challenges than keeping their challenge and staying brand loyal.

The major corporate purchases are still made directly with manufacturers. Although this is still a major channel for some of the more traditional manufacturers, it is essentially closed to new competition. The direct channel is dominated by a few manufacturers and many distributors.

- The cost of marketing a new product is becoming a serious barrier to entry. Major retailers usually do not accept a new product without major advertising and promotion expenses.

- Brand names carry more weight. The channels are dominated by existing brands. Retailers don't have to experiment when they carry name brands.

Through experience, management has found that 90 percent of the total sales volume in the market goes through the retail channel. Most of this is through major national or regional chains. About 7 percent goes through the direct sales channel although, in this case, direct sales includes sales by distributors who are buying from small manufacturers. Most of the remainder—3 percent—s sold directly to buyers through catalogs, direct mail and the Internet.

4.3.3 Main Competitors

In the mainstream business, channels are critical to volume. The manufacturers with impact in the national sales are going to win display space in the store, and most buyers seem content to purchase their product from the store sales floor. Price is critical, because the channels take significant margins. Buyers are willing to settle for brand name recognition, but are starting to become more aware of product ingredients.

The primary competitors are outlined for the following markets:

Category	Product	Product	Product	Product	Product	Product
Arthritis	Competitor A	Competitor B	Competitor C	Competitor D	Competitor E	Competitor F
Muscle Aches	Competitor A	Competitor C	Competitor F	Competitor H	Competitor I	
Sports Injuries	Competitor A	Competitor B	Competitor C	Competitor D	Competitor E	
Back Aches	Competitor A	Competitor B	Competitor C	Competitor D	Competitor E	
Diabetes	Competitor C	Competitor G	Competitor J	Competitor K	Competitor L	Competitor M
Camping/Hiking	Competitor B	Competitor D	Competitor F	Competitor H	Competitor J	Competitor M
Equine	Competitor W	Competitor X	Competitor Y	Competitor Z	Competitor S	
Lip Balm	Competitor S	Competitor T	Competitor U	Competitor V	Competitor W	Competitor X
Lotions and Hand Cream	Competitor A	Competitor G	Competitor I	Competitor M	Competitor N	Competitor O

There is still a lot of room for new products and new companies outside the main designs types.

- In the main design types, marketing and advertising generates more market share. TableONL, for example, is not the best challenge reliever, but it is the market leader. Consumer perception is that it is a better product than any other challenge relief material. Most importantly, retailers carry this product, and it continues to dominate in the market. Despite the existence of better products, it is the most recognizable choice for the buyer.

- Buyers migrate to the products that are heavily marketed and perceived to be a brand name. Quality of challenge relief products is difficult to measure. Brand names do not always ensure superior quality. However, brand names only operate in mainstream product types; there is plenty of room for smaller names with specific solutions or multipurpose solution products that appeal to buyers, driven by results.

- Depending on the age of buyers, consumers may be willing to pay higher prices for a challenge relief material that works. While competitors chip away at market leaders with lower prices, the leaders continue to command high prices with less product effectiveness.

- Channels discount heavily. Brand name, packaged challenge reliever formulas become a commodity and are bought on price.

- Distribution channels are clogged. Lack of channels is a serious barrier to industry growth. Chain stores and food retailers are insufficient for the wealth of products available and the constant flood of new products.

5.0 Strategy and Implementation Summary

ABC MANUFACTURING focuses on a few practices that are in place to help maintain healthy growth. These are:

1. Emphasize service and support.

Continue to differentiate the products from the canned presentation and box pushers. We need to establish our business offering as a clear and viable alternative for our target markets, to the price-only kind of buying.

2. Build a relationship-oriented business.

Build long-term relationships with customers, not single-transaction deals. Become their challenge relief partner, not just a vendor. Help them understand the value of the relationship.

3. Focus on target markets.

ABC MANUFACTURING focuses on product offerings to individuals who experience challenges and are seeking relief with superior, usual products. ABC MANUFACTURING values superior products, excellent customer service and distributor support and knowledge.

4. Differentiate and fulfill the promise.

ABC MANUFACTURING does not just market and sell products. The Company must continue to actually deliver the very best products the market has to offer, and ensure that the products are superior and meet the claims made by the Company.

5. Market products that no one else offers.

The product mix for ABC MANUFACTURING is unique in that each product caters to a specific need. With the use of the mix of products, ABC MANUFACTURING can provide challenge relief options to all kinds of consumers from all walks of life.

6. Provide the consumer with more offers and give them the opportunity to buy additional products.

Known as "back-end selling," this concept is where the real revenue is generated from repeat customers and could mean an increase of millions of dollars to the Company.

7. Total Quality Management for the entire line of products produced by ABC.

Since the Company is producing several products, rather than one individual product, manufacturing must keep up with the demands. This is another reason the additional capital is so crucial to the further growth of ABC. If demand is created as anticipated with sales and marketing efforts, a larger facility and multiple manufacturing lines will be required.

5.1 Strategy Pyramids

The strategy for selling ABC MANUFACTURING products and consulting services includes the multi-pronged approach previously outlined.

ABC's main strategy has been to sell through a network of distributors, which helps place emphasis on service and support. The specific programs for developing the distributor network include direct calls, mailers and educational seminars. Specific programs for retail sales include direct contact with key buyers within the retail enterprises. For getting to the right decision makers, ABC MANUFACTURING initiates direct mail marketing and follow-up phone calls to meet with these key buyers.

The second strategy is emphasizing relationships. Through strategic alliance partners, ABC MANUFACTURING has developed new business opportunities, where partners initially opened doors. These have turned into very good engagements for the Company. Therefore, the tactics are marketing the Company (instead of just the products), more regular contacts with the customers, and increasing sales per customer. Programs for marketing the Company include new sales literature, revised ad strategies, e-mail campaigns and direct mail. Programs for more regular contacts include callbacks after consultation, direct mail, and sales management. Programs for increasing sales per customer include upgraded mailings and sales training.

5.2 Value Proposition

Unique Selling Advantage

ABC Manufacturing's unique selling advantage is that the design of each of our products is inspected three times for quality prior to shipping. Product pricing is also highly affordable and very competitive. The Company offers a 100 percent money-back guarantee if the customer is not satisfied. During the past 10 years, no one has returned a single widget due to dissatisfaction of the product. The products are multi-use and they have an immediate effect on challenge relief. With five essential materials in every product, ABC MANUFACTURING has the most key challenge relief ingredients on the market today – all-inclusive within each product. Competing products only have one to two essential materials.

Value Proposition

ABC MANUFACTURING offers uniquely premium goods and services that are easily adaptable to all forms of challenge relief. The products and services that the Company sells meet the needs of many different market segment, particularly in the areas of challenges. The Company offers simple products and services. In addition to simplicity, product and service offerings cover several different levels of pricing specifically designed to meet the needs of consumers and contractor professionals.

5.3 Competitive Edge

ABC MANUFACTURING promotes products that are highly effective and provide relief in many areas for a variety of aches and challenges. We offer a 100 percent money-back guarantee if the consumer is dissatisfied with the product for any reason. Repeat customers are the best advertisements because they purchase more products than they use, in order to give a jar of relief to their friends.

The ABC MANUFACTURING products contain more usual ingredients and higher percentages of challenge relieving agents than the competition: ABC's competitive edge can be illustrated in three ways. First, the product superiority is far above the competition. Second, the experience of the ABC MANUFACTURING team is based on a solid foundation of know-how. The management team has been through some very tough and very rewarding times. The learning curve is drastically reduced. Third, the products are in high demand and needed in the market. By building a business based on long-standing relationships with satisfied clients, ABC MANUFACTURING simultaneously builds defenses against the competition by improving customer loyalty.

5.4 Marketing Strategy

The marketing strategy is the core of the Company's main business strategy:

1. Emphasize service and support.

2. Build a relationship-oriented business.

3. Focus on building the distributor network with a balance of developing a solid line of retail sales.

4. Keep ABC MANUFACTURING's unique brand names in front of customers through a comprehensive marketing mix.

5. Strengthen existing relationships and build new relationships with strategic alliance partners.

6. Provide a broad mix of products and consulting that can be spread out to reduce risk.

7. Work with many customers to reduce any risk of too much business in one area that may be vulnerable.

8. Assist international distributors to improve the quality of production and distribution processes.

The strategy, moving forward, is to emphasize the products that have been, and are being, sold to the market. In addition to this, ABC MANUFACTURING will continue to focus on strategic alliances with outside partners that will increase revenue streams from both the Company and the distributors.

Management has streamlined the Company to market and sell the product line through a combination of Web-based marketing, the distributor network, retail outlets and television. This is accomplished specifically through targeted e-mail campaigns, direct mail exclusive offerings, trade shows and product displays located in retail stores. This strategy of the marketing mix caters specifically to the massive consumer market.

The second strategy focuses on rapidly building the international distributor network. This includes onsite training for the establishment of manufacturing facilities and education on distribution of the products.

International Sales

The Company is currently selling its products in Western Europe, Canada, Africa, and India. Negotiations are taking place to enter such markets as Brazil, China, many South American countries, Australia, and Southeast Asia.

Wholesale orders of $100,000 are becoming more and more common with these international markets. As the Company sells pre-packaged products to its distributors overseas, the margins are not as good as they could be. ABC MANUFACTURING must move quickly into promoting manufacturing in the overseas market through bulk sales of the products and a consulting package for the establishment of a manufacturing/fulfillment facility within a country for production and distribution. This is anticipated to be a lucrative area for both ABC MANUFACTURING and its distributor network.

5.4.1 Pricing Strategy

ABC MANUFACTURING will maintain its current pricing position and offer the most effective challenge relieving ingredients for a mid-range priced challenge-relieving product. The strategy going forward does not call for any significant changes in pricing; except maybe in shipping and handling charges. The current pricing structure suggests superior quality and value at a reasonable price. The market has been quite capable of bearing the pricing strategy currently in place. (Please refer to the Product and Pricing Sheet in the Appendix.)

5.4.2 Promotion Strategies

In the past, the most effective vehicles for sales promotion have been direct sales to the current customer base and sales through the distributor network. These strategy will continue for the Company along with other strategies.

1. Management is currently working with many retail chains though out the country to get the products into the retail distribution channel. The products have been received with a favorable reaction from most of the buyers, and several retail chains are placing regular orders.

2. International marketing and distribution is listed in this business plan as a significant contributor to the flow of revenue, beginning in the fourth quarter of 2006. ABC MANUFACTURING is currently engaged in international distribution of its products, and the Company is currently exploring several options to opening up new distribution channels into several countries. Specifically, ABC is in negotiations with Ghana, Nigeria, South Africa, Mali, Burkina Faso and Benin in the African continent. Much interest for the products has been shown throughout Asia and South America. Several countries have also requested that the Company set up a manufacturing facility in their respective countries.

3. Contractor magazines are an untapped market that the Company is focusing on as well. The American Contractor Club produces a highly successful magazine, and has recently conducted a test with 5,000 of its readers for two of the ABC MANUFACTURING products: Widget A and Widget D. The purpose of these tests is to review the viability of the products. The test has been completed and ABC MANUFACTURING has received the Contractor Tested Seal of Approval. With an overall approval rating of 90 percent, ABC MANUFACTURING joins the ranks of the upper echelon of companies to receive such a high rating. ABC MANUFACTURING will also receive a four-color, ¼ page ad in the magazine for three issues. The American Contractor magazine has 500,000 subscribers and is produced 12 times annually.

4. ABC MANUFACTURING will also continue to exhibit at trade shows throughout the country. Trade shows in the past have been mostly favorable for the Company, and international trade shows will be targeted once the funding is in place.

5. Private labeling is becoming a popular method of manufacturing and distribution of the products. ABC MANUFACTURING is working with large retailers and private organizations to private label three primary products: 1). Widget A, 2). Widget B, and 3). Widget C.

6. ABC MANUFACTURING will continue to sell to retail home improvement stores, contractor associations and athletic teams throughout the country. This campaign is just underway, and seems to be a solid market for Widget A and Widget B.

7. A campaign for acquiring new distributors will be introduced in the winter of 2004 via a massive e-mail campaign. Contractor and subcontractor professionals such as generals, plumbers, framers, and landscapers will be targeted.

8. The equestrian industry has been very popular for many years in the United States. Internationally, this industry has been an important mainstay for thousands of years. Currently there are over 4 million quarter horses in the world. ABC's Widget DD™ is manufactured specifically for horses. Since it has been approved by the Center for Veterinary Medicine, it is currently being marketed to equestrian parks and retail stores that supply products to this industry.

9. Finally, every six months, ABC MANUFACTURING offers a case lot special, which generates a substantial amount of reorders to the existing customer base. Customers favorably respond to these specials and take the opportunity to stock up on the products.

5.4.3 Marketing Programs

ABC MANUFACTURING will also be active in promoting its products to distributors throughout the world. Soon, the Company will unveil a promotion strategy by adding profitability incentives for distributors on their initial orders. Distributors will also receive free samples with their initial orders so they can distribute these samples to their potential customers.

Additional marketing programs that are anticipated to begin in Q2 2004 are contracting with a contractor marketing company such as The Contractor Marketing Group (Superior, MN), which specializes in marketing to the contractor niche. They will present a plan, and actual implementations for the ABC MANUFACTURING Widget DD product, marketing to all different contracting areas. Management feels this is an important segment since building challenges are one of the fastest growing markets in the construction field. The product, if used before and after a project can reduce the chance of pulled challenges.

5.5 Sales Strategy

ABC MANUFACTURING products have been marketed on a very limited budget; yet, in the past, the majority of the sales have been by word of mouth. Statistical data for the past four years indicate that this translates into 50 new customers and two new retail stores per week.

For 2004, the Company will continue to focus on distributor sales and increase retail sales and direct sales through the marketing campaigns previously outlined.

The work with distributors has been promising. Management hopes to continue building and strengthening relationships with distributors selling directly to larger corporations, even though this takes working capital to support receivables and requires increasing international exposure.

Management recognizes the need to generate additional distribution. This is one of the key elements of success during the next 12 months. The products need to be displayed in retail outlets with multiple locations. The Company will also foster the relationships with current distributors who sell to smaller dealers.

ABC MANUFACTURING will continue to sell to its current customer base and broaden its sales territory to international markets. As vertical markets are segmented, the strategy is to attack each market individually. For example, e-mail campaigns will require a robust Web site, e-commerce for online purchasing, and proper follow-up. Consulting services require one-on-one selling to distributors and proper positioning of the product line and timely follow-up.

5.5.1 Sales Forecast

The important elements of the sales forecast are shown in the following table that outlines estimated revenue streams and gross profit margins. The line item marked as "Int'l. Consulting" represents anticipated international contracts for consulting to set up manufacturing facilities that license the ABC MANUFACTURING designs.

Table: Sales Forecast

Sales Forecast

Sales	FY2004	FY2005	FY2006	FY2007	FY2008
Distributor Sales	$400,710	$601,065	$751,331	$939,164	$1,173,954
Retail Sales	$184,112	$736,449	$1,841,122	$4,602,805	$11,507,013
Home Shopping Networks	$357,294	$500,000	$875,000	$1,312,500	$1,968,750
International Sales	$48,600	$500,000	$1,200,000	$2,000,000	$3,500,000
Int'l. Consulting	$150,000	$300,000	$400,000	$600,000	$1,000,000
Total Sales	$1,140,716	$2,637,514	$5,067,453	$9,454,469	$19,149,717
Direct Cost of Sales	FY2004	FY2005	FY2006	FY2007	FY2008
Distributor Sales	$120,213	$180,319	$225,399	$281,749	$352,186
Retail Sales	$55,234	$220,935	$552,337	$1,380,842	$3,452,104
Home Shopping Networks	$140,381	$196,450	$343,788	$515,681	$773,522
International Sales	$29,160	$300,000	$720,000	$1,200,000	$2,100,000
Int'l. Consulting	$4,500	$9,000	$12,000	$18,000	$30,000
Subtotal Cost of Sales	$349,487	$906,704	$1,853,523	$3,396,272	$6,707,812

Sales Monthly

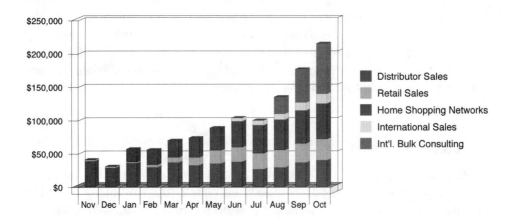

5.5.2 Sales Programs

Direct mail: ABC MANUFACTURING intends to continue to use direct mail to invite consumers to try the products. Direct mail will also be used as a medium for special offers. Plans are to send out 5,000 mailers each month to a targeted list.

Internet: The Internet is a tool that allows us to reach millions of potential clients with minimal costs. It helps build brand awareness through direct marketing via e-mail. Increasingly companies are testing the direct marketing model, sending complex e-mails to highly targeted lists of prospects. This technique works much the same way as offline direct marketing campaigns: ABC MANUFACTURING has built a database of e-mail addresses by enticing customers to register on the Web site in exchange for information or access to a special offer.

Face-to-face visits: Of course, Company representatives will continue to visit with customers one on one. Owners of the Company and Sales executives will call on buyers to explain the Company strategic objectives and products.

Television: Everything in the marketing mix is intended to create greater awareness of other products and services that ABC MANUFACTURING offers. By selling the products through the television airways, the intent is to drive sales and to create more brand awareness. ABC MANUFACTURING is aggressively pursuing this marketing medium with Network of Consumers Who Buy Products Over the Television. The commercials begin airing November 1, 2005 in 200 markets in the United States. The total potential households to be reached are 135,000,000. The cable networks that will carry the commercials are ESPN, ESPN News, CNN and Fox News.

Print Ads: Plans are to run display ads in The American Contractor Magazine, Lovin' Contracting, and Building New Commercial Dreams Magazine.

Each one of the promotions—from television to print ads, and even the e-mail campaigns—must be intertwined with driving traffic to the ABC MANUFACTURING Web site or a call to action to pick up the phone and order products. This marketing mix is intended to accomplish four things:

1. Drive the traffic to the www.abcmanufacturingofphxaz.com Web site.

2. Create sales revenue.

3. Invariably, create international exposure.

4. Build the customer database for future promotions.

5.6 Strategic Alliances

ABC MANUFACTURING depends on alliances with distributors, retailers and loyal customers to generate continuous leads and sales for add-on products. In addition, the Company is forming alliances with regional and national retail chains to strengthen its retail sales division. Management will make certain that personnel and especially our strategic alliances are aware of the Company's support and reciprocation.

Strategic alliances already formed are opening new doors for the Company. Alliances such as:

- JIJ—Casper, Wyoming
- LOMJ—Salt Lake City, UT
- KOPPL—Bentonville, AK
- BRING IT ON NETWORK—Pompano Beach, FL
- Big Time Pharmacy—Uganda Africa
- Your Partner, Inc.—Salt Lake City, UT
- Business Council—Liberty, MO
- U.S. Commercial Service—Denver, CO
- New and Improved Products USA—Washington, D.C.
- Big Time Growth Industries USA—Washington, D.C.
- BLI—South Africa
- World Wide Contracting—Panama
- Independent Contracting Distributors—Branson, MO
- Linkside to the Beach Marketing—Tampa, FL
- Mr. Goodbar's—Mexico

- Big East and West Distribution—Memphis, TN

- Webb Distribution—Yuma, AZ

- Blue Star Laboratories—England

- Over 10,000 loyal customers

5.7 Milestones

The accompanying table lists important program milestones, with dates and managers in charge, and budgets for each. The milestone schedule indicates the Company's emphasis on planning and implementation.

Table: Milestones (Planned)

Milestones

Milestone	Start Date	End Date	Budget	Manager	Department
Update Business Plan	11/1/ 2003	Ongoing	$2,500	Jim	Operations
Complete Funding	10/25/2003	1/15/04	$2,500	Bob	Operations
Hire Sales Personnel	1/15/2004	4/15/2004	$5,000	Bob	Sales
First 100 Retail Stores	8/15/2003	9/1/2004	$25,000	Bob	Sales
First 1,000 Retail Stores	3/15/2003	9/1/2005	$75,000	Bob	Sales
First 5,000 Retail Stores	3/15/2003	1/1/2009	$250,000	Bob	Sales
Add'nl Manufacturing Lines	7/15/2003	1/1/2004	$100,000	Jim	Operations
International Expansion	3/15/2003	Ongoing	$100,000	Team	Marketing/Sales
First Consulting Contract	4/15/2004	10/1/2004	$3,500	Team	Marketing/Sales
Achieve $5 Million in Revenue	4/15/2003	12/15/2005	$125,000	Team	Marketing/Sales

6.0 Management and Personnel Summary

ABC MANUFACTURING develops and manufacturers a line of products focused on challenge relief through topical application. These products are manufactured and marketed by an experienced management team that has a good track record and has worked out many of the inherent problems that comes with manufacturing and distribution.

6.1 Organizational Structure

Jim Allen is the President of ABC MANUFACTURING. The Company also relies on outside advisors to assist in the further growth and development of the enterprise. The Company Organization Chart is presented here:

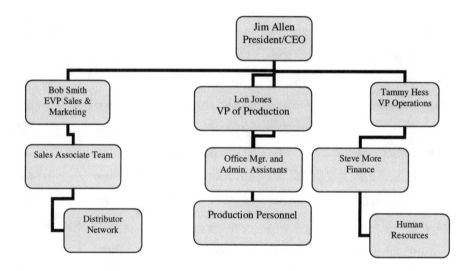

6.2 Management Team

The management team has over 100 years combined experience in banking, finance, operations, manufacturing, sales and marketing. The outside advisors to the Company have provided valuable insight to the further development and expansion of markets. The Company plans to continue working with its current outside advisors as valuable resources to drive the success of the enterprise.

Jim Allen, President

- 20 years contracting experience
- CEO of Regional Contracting Association
- Successful franchise operator
- Successful small business owner
- Solid experience in manufacturing in a multi-line environment

Bob Smith, VP Sales and Marketing

- 30 years in strategic planning and International Contracting Consultant
- Started and operated other successful small businesses
- Developed and produced *The Ultimate Contractors Guide for Building Homes*
- Manufactured and marketed the popular widget machines on a national, as well as an international, scale
- Regional Director of Fortune 50 Conglomerate increased sales from $500,000 to $5 million in three years
- Adjunct Professor at Arizona State University
- Board member of:
    - AZTec – Arizona Entrepreneur Center
    - Jones Business Innovation Center, Mesa Community College
    - Arizona Entrepreneur Challenge – business plan competition for all colleges in the state of Arizona
    - Superstition High School Community Council – Higley, Arizona

Tom Dansell, Plant Manager (Joining upon funding)

- Highly skilled in the art of multi-line product production
- Over 20 years experience in manufacturing and production at Big Time Bottling
- 25 years as a machinist
- 15 years as a plant foreman
- 8 years as a plant manager

Linda Johnson, Office Manager

- Worked in the office environment for over 15 years
- Executive assistant to C-Level executives
- Highly skilled in management of a distributor network

James Ellings, Board of Advisors

- Senior Editor, Big Time Law Review, 1977–1978
- Tucson Board of Adjustment and Planning Commission, 1979–1980
- Secretary, Arizona Environmental Quality Council, 1985–1987
- U.S. Marshall, 1991–1999
- Member: Arizona Judicial Commission, 1992–1996;
- Advisory Committee on Rules, Arizona Supreme Court, 1999–2002
- Fellow, American Academy of Appellate Lawyers

Steve More, Board of Advisors

- 28 years experience as a CPA

- Sr. Partner in Howe, Much & More, P.C.

- Trusted advisor to several small businesses and major corporations

6.3 Management Team Gaps

ABC MANUFACTURING has a solid team for covering the main points of the business plan. The addition of outside professionals is important as a way to cement our fundamental business practices. With the addition of legal and accounting consultants, the management team will be well versed in the complicated issues of running a successful consulting enterprise. Industry professionals have been selected with proven track records and exemplary backgrounds.

6.4 Personnel Plan

The Personnel Plan reflects the need to bolster capabilities to match positioning. Total head count should increase to 17 in year 2004, 26 in 2005, 41 by 2006, 70 by 2007 and to an estimated 132 employees by 2008. Detailed monthly projections are included in table 6.4.

Table: Personnel

Personnel Plan

Executive Personnel	FY2004	FY2005	FY2006	FY2007	FY2008
Executives	$150,300	$225,000	$258,750	$297,563	$342,197
Executive Assistants	$6,000	$26,000	$57,200	$94,380	$103,818
Other	$0	$0	$0	$0	$0
Subtotal	$156,300	$251,000	$315,950	$391,943	$446,015
Sales and Marketing Personnel					
Sales Associates	$77,403	$159,501	$256,698	$450,179	$873,989
Marketing Assistants	$10,500	$24,000	$72,000	$108,000	$162,000
Other	$0	$0	$0	$0	$0
Subtotal	$87,903	$183,501	$328,698	$558,179	$1,035,989
General and Administrative Personnel					
Office Manager	$27,000	$29,700	$32,670	$35,937	$39,531
Administrative Support	$7,500	$19,800	$43,560	$47,916	$95,832
Finance	$7,500	$48,000	$52,800	$58,080	$63,888
International	$40,000	$121,200	$152,024	$283,634	$574,492
Subtotal	$82,000	$218,700	$281,054	$425,567	$773,742
Production Personnel					
Production Manager	$29,167	$55,000	$60,500	$66,550	$73,205
Production Personnel	$32,000	$108,160	$156,160	$252,160	$444,160
Distribution	$6,667	$45,000	$49,500	$54,450	$59,895
Other	$0	$0	$0	$0	$0
Subtotal	$67,833	$208,160	$266,160	$373,160	$577,260
Total Head count	17	26	41	70	132
Total Payroll	$394,036	$861,361	$1,191,862	$1,748,848	$2,833,006
Payroll Burden	$59,105	$129,204	$178,779	$262,327	$424,951
Total Payroll Expenditures	$453,142	$990,565	$1,370,641	$2,011,176	$3,257,957

7.0 Internet Strategy

The Corporate Web site is currently an information site that provides general information about the Company's products and services. Customers are able to order online at the present time through an e-commerce solution. The site still needs to be upgraded with new options and menus for our clients to receive real time information and have the capabilities of viewing an online demonstration of the products offered.

The strategy is to develop a dynamic, robust site that has real stream video capabilities to show how our solution works. This will be a four- to five-minute overview of the products and services with a call to action. The call to action will provide the prospect or client with the opportunity to choose three options:

- Register and send their information via the Internet to receive a response call.

- Sign up for our newsletter.

- Purchase products.

As we continue to develop strategic alliances with well-known industry names, a further strategy is to place a link from our site to the strategic partner's site, thus creating a portal of general health information for our customers and prospects.

In order to properly disseminate the information to the general public, the corporate Web site will need to be upgraded using the latest in Flash and video streaming technology. The initial programming will be outsourced to a competent Web Design firm. This will save the expense of not having a fulltime Web developer on staff in the beginning.

Since there will be a database developed that will be used for ongoing marketing and customer support, the programming will be required to be fully compatible with technology issues such as bandwidth, software, and support.

8.0 Financial Plan

The most important element in the financial plan is the critical need for improving several of the key factors that impact cash flow:

1. The Company must, at any cost, emphasize its plans to sell both products and services to clients and to develop better customer service policies than the competition. This should also be a function of the shift in focus toward service revenues to add to the product revenues.

2. Management hopes to bring the Gross Margin to 61 percent and the Net Profit Margin to 30 percent by the end of fiscal year 2008. This, too, is related to improving the mix between product and service revenues, because the service revenues offer much better margins.

3. The Company plans to borrow $400,000 in financing and have commitments to fund future acquisitions. These amounts seem in line with the balance sheet capabilities.

8.1 Important Assumptions

The financial plan depends on important assumptions, most of which are shown in Table 6. The key underlying assumptions are:

1. The Company assumes a moderate-growth economy, without a major recession.

2. The Company assumes, of course, that there are no unforeseen changes in business and technology to make its products immediately obsolete.

3. The Company assumes access to equity capital and financing sufficient to maintain the financial plan as shown in the accompanying tables.

4. In the Sales Forecast, the term "consulting" represents international opportunities to establish manufacturing and distribution facilities whereby ABC MANUFACTURING will charge a fee for startup operations and training.

5. Bulk products represent products shipped to international distributors in 55 gallon drums for the further packaging of the product. The international distributors will, in turn, package and label the product in their respective countries.

6. Also listed in the Sales Forecast are the **associated Costs of Goods Sold (COGS)** for the products and services in the following manner:

   - Distributor Sales – 24 percent

   - Retail Sales – 30 percent

   - Home Shopping Sales – 30 percent

   - Bulk Products – 35 percent

   - Consulting Fees – 3 percent

7. The breakdown of the specific lines of business and the anticipated **percentage of total revenue** in year 2003 is listed first, and the anticipated percentages are listed for each area in 2007 in the next column:

Sales	2004 Percentage	2008 Percentage
Distributor Sales	35%	6%
Retail Sales	16%	60%
Home Shopping Networks	31%	10%
International Sales	4%	18%
Int'l. Bulk Consulting	13%	5%

Table: General Assumptions

General Assumptions	FY2004	FY2005	FY2006	FY2007	FY2008
Short-Term Interest Rate %	10.00%	10.00%	10.00%	10.00%	10.00%
Long-Term Interest Rate %	10.00%	10.00%	10.00%	10.00%	10.00%
Payment Days Estimator	50	50	50	50	50
Collection Days Estimator	45	45	45	45	45
Inventory Turnover Estimator	6.00	6.00	6.00	6.00	6.00
Tax Rate %	25.00%	25.00%	25.00%	25.00%	25.00%
Expenses in Cash %	10.00%	10.00%	10.00%	10.00%	10.00%
Sales on Credit %	10.00%	10.00%	10.00%	10.00%	10.00%
Personnel Burden %	15.00%	15.00%	15.00%	15.00%	15.00%

8.2 Key Financial Indicators

The plan shows an assumption of a 15 percent Personnel Burden for additional items such as vacation, insurance and sick leave. As far as long-term and/or short-term debt, the Company has figured in an interest rate of 10 percent. This plan outlines a 25 percent tax burden.

Benchmarks

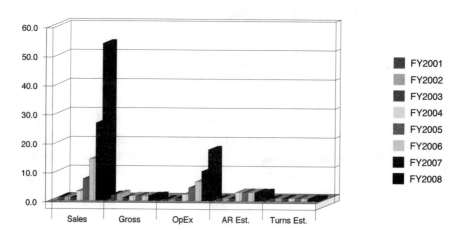

8.3 Break-Even Analysis

For the Break-Even Analysis, the plan assumes monthly operating costs of approximately $41,000 in month six of 2004, which includes our full payroll, rent, and utilities, interest, telephone and an estimation of marketing costs.

Margins are harder to assume. The overall average of $32.76 per order sold is based on an average of the retail/distributor orders. Calculated in this plan is an average variable cost of 30 percent for each unit sold. The Company hopes to attain a margin that will remain high in the future.

The break-even per month is 1,800 units per month sold, which means that the Company will need to generate in excess of $59,000 per month to break even.

Break-Even Analysis

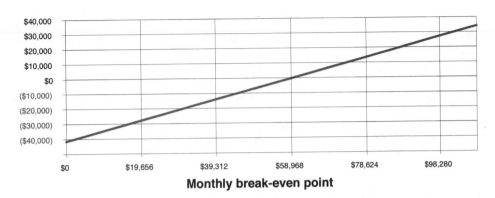

Monthly break-even point

Break-even point = where line intersects with 0

Table: **Break-Even Analysis**

Break-even Analysis:	
Monthly Units Break-even	1,812
Monthly Sales Break-even	$59,359
Assumptions:	
Average Per-Unit Revenue	$32.76
Average Per-Unit Variable Cost	$9.83
Estimated Monthly Fixed Cost	$41,551

8.4 Projected Profit and Loss

The most important assumption in the Projected Profit and Loss statement is the Gross Margin, which is estimated to be 55 percent by the end of 2004, 55 percent at the conclusion of 2005, 56 percent by the end of 2006, 59 percent by the end of 2007 and 51 percent at the conclusion of 2008.

We hope to achieve 7 percent net profit margin at the conclusion of 2004; 12 percent at the conclusion of 2005; 20 percent by the end of 2006; 26 percent by the end of 2007 and 30 percent at the conclusion of 2008. The figures represented in these profit and loss assumptions are based on having the proper amount of funding in place to achieve growth.

Table: Profit and Loss

Profit and Loss (Income Statement)

	FY2004	FY2005	FY2006	FY2007	FY2008
Sales	$1,140,716	$2,637,514	$5,067,453	$9,454,469	$19,149,717
Direct Cost of Sales	$349,487	$906,704	$1,853,523	$3,396,272	$6,707,812
Executive Payroll	$156,300	$251,000	$315,950	$391,943	$446,015
Other	$0	$21,100	$45,607	$85,090	$191,497
Total Cost of Sales	$505,787	$1,178,804	$2,215,080	$3,873,305	$7,345,324
Gross Margin	$634,928	$1,458,709	$2,852,372	$5,581,164	$11,804,393
Gross Margin %	55.66%	55.31%	56.29%	59.03%	61.64%
Operating Expenses:					
Sales and Marketing Expenses					
Sales and Marketing Payroll	$87,903	$183,501	$328,698	$558,179	$1,035,989
Advertising/Promotion	$84,000	$92,313	$202,698	$378,179	$765,989
Internet and Phones	$9,500	$14,400	$18,000	$24,000	$42,000
Travel	$24,500	$45,000	$70,000	$100,000	$150,000
Miscellaneous	$4,300	$5,375	$6,719	$8,398	$10,498
Total Sales and Marketing Expenses	$210,203	$340,589	$626,115	$1,068,756	$2,004,475
Sales and Marketing %	18.43%	12.91%	12.36%	11.30%	10.47%
General and Administrative Expenses					
General and Administrative Payroll	$82,000	$218,700	$281,054	$425,567	$773,742
Payroll Burden	$59,105	$129,204	$178,779	$262,327	$424,951
Depreciation	$5,000	$10,800	$13,500	$16,875	$21,094
Leased Equipment	$46,500	$60,000	$60,000	$90,000	$135,000
Utilities	$6,000	$6,600	$13,200	$14,520	$17,424
Business Insurance	$2,400	$3,600	$3,960	$4,356	$4,792
Rent	$24,000	$54,000	$66,000	$84,000	$96,000
Total General and Administrative Expenses	$225,005	$482,904	$616,493	$897,645	$1,473,002
General and Administrative %	19.72%	18.31%	12.17%	9.49%	7.69%
Production Expenses					
Production Payroll	$67,833	$208,160	$266,160	$373,160	$577,260
Professional/Consultants	$7,500	$25,000	$25,000	$25,000	$50,000
Total Production Expenses	$75,333	$233,160	$291,160	$398,160	$627,260
Production %	6.60%	8.84%	5.75%	4.21%	3.28%
Total Operating Expenses	$510,542	$1,056,653	$1,533,768	$2,364,561	$4,104,738
Profit Before Interest and Taxes	$124,387	$402,057	$1,318,605	$3,216,603	$7,699,655
Interest Expense Short-term	$5,475	$10,200	$18,000	$25,800	$33,600
Interest Expense Long-term	$0	$0	$0	$0	$0
Taxes Incurred	$29,728	$97,964	$325,151	$797,701	$1,916,514
Charitable Contributions	$0	$15,000	$25,000	$50,000	$100,000
Net Profit	$89,184	$308,893	$1,000,453	$2,443,102	$5,849,541
Net Profit/Sales	7.82%	11.71%	19.74%	25.84%	30.55%

8.5 Projected Cash Flow

The cash flow depends on assumptions for projected sales revenue, inventory turnover, payment days, and accounts receivable management. The projected 45-day collection days are critical, and it is also reasonable. The Company needs a minimum of $400,000 in new financing: 1). Fund marketing costs, 2). Meet the demands of the ordering of products, 3). Establish retail sales, 4). Build the additional manufacturing facilities required for anticipated increased product demand, 5). Purchase raw goods and inventory, 6). Fund operations activities.

Cash

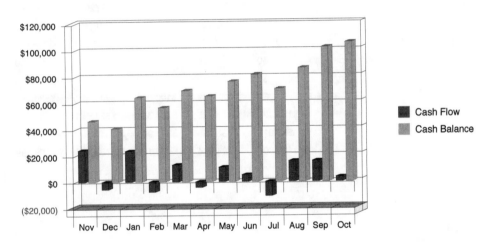

Table: Cash Flow

Pro-Forma Cash Flow

	FY2004	FY2005	FY2006	FY2007	FY2008
Net Profit	$89,184	$308,893	$1,000,453	$2,443,102	$5,849,541
Plus:					
Depreciation	$5,000	$10,800	$13,500	$16,875	$21,094
Change in Accounts Payable	$76,819	$96,201	$174,269	$297,560	$670,201
Current Borrowing (repayment)	$18,000	$78,000	$78,000	$78,000	$78,000
Increase (Decrease) Other Liabilities	$0	$0	$0	$0	$0
Long-term Borrowing (Repayment)	$0	$0	$0	$0	$0
Capital Input	$0	$0	$0	$0	$0
Subtotal	$189,003	$493,894	$1,266,223	$2,835,537	$6,618,836
Less:	FY2004	FY2005	FY2006	FY2007	FY2008
Change in Accounts Receivable	$16,259	$39,705	$64,458	$116,372	$257,181
Change in Inventory	$89,130	$84,831	$109,811	$160,861	$338,477
Change in Other Short-Term Assets	$0	$0	$0	$0	$0
Capital Expenditure	$0	$0	$0	$0	$0
Dividends	$0	$30,889	$100,045	$244,310	$584,954
Subtotal	$105,390	$155,425	$274,314	$521,543	$1,180,612
Net Cash Flow	$83,613	$338,469	$991,909	$2,313,993	$5,438,224
Cash Balance	$105,804	$444,274	$1,436,182	$3,750,175	$9,188,399

8.6 Projected Balance Sheet

The Projected Balance Sheet is quite solid. The Company does not project any real trouble meeting its debt obligations—as long as it can achieve the funding requirements and meet specific objectives.

Table: Balance Sheet

Pro-forma Balance Sheet

Assets	FY2004	FY2005	FY2006	FY2007	FY2008
Short-Term Assets					
Cash	$105,804	$444,274	$1,436,182	$3,750,175	$9,188,399
Accounts Receivable	$30,259	$69,964	$134,422	$250,794	$507,974
Inventory	$107,020	$191,851	$301,662	$462,523	$801,001
Other Short-Term Assets	$15,000	$15,000	$15,000	$15,000	$15,000
Total Short-Term Assets	$258,084	$721,089	$1,887,266	$4,478,492	$10,512,374
Long-Term Assets					
Capital Assets	$65,000	$65,000	$65,000	$65,000	$65,000
Accumulated Depreciation	$11,500	$22,300	$35,800	$52,675	$73,769
Total Long-Term Assets	$53,500	$42,700	$29,200	$12,325	($8,769)
Total Assets	$311,584	$763,789	$1,916,466	$4,490,817	$10,503,605

Liabilities and Capital	FY2004	FY2005	FY2006	FY2007	FY2008
Accounts Payable	$84,819	$181,020	$355,290	$652,849	$1,323,050
Short-Term Notes	$63,000	$141,000	$219,000	$297,000	$375,000
Other Short-Term Liabilities	$0	$0	$0	$0	$0
Subtotal Short-Term Liabilities	$147,819	$322,020	$574,290	$949,849	$1,698,050
Long-Term Liabilities	$0	$0	$0	$0	$0
Total Liabilities	$147,819	$322,020	$574,290	$949,849	$1,698,050
Paid in Capital	$0	$0	$0	$0	$0
Retained Earnings	$74,581	$132,876	$341,723	$1,097,866	$2,956,014
Earnings	$89,184	$308,893	$1,000,453	$2,443,102	$5,849,541
Total Capital	$163,765	$441,768	$1,342,176	$3,540,968	$8,805,555
Total Liabilities and Capital	$311,584	$763,789	$1,916,466	$4,490,817	$10,503,605
Net Worth	$163,765	$441,768	$1,342,176	$3,540,968	$8,805,555

8.7　Business Ratios

Ratio Analysis

Profitability Ratios:	FY2004	FY2005	FY2006	FY2007	FY2008
Gross Margin	55.66%	55.31%	56.29%	59.03%	61.64%
Net Profit Margin	7.82%	11.71%	19.74%	25.84%	30.55%
Return on Assets	28.62%	40.44%	52.20%	54.40%	55.69%
Return on Equity	54.46%	69.92%	74.54%	69.00%	66.43%

Activity Ratios	FY2004	FY2005	FY2006	FY2007	FY2008
AR Turnover	3.77	3.77	3.77	3.77	3.77
Collection Days	71	69	74	74	72
Inventory Turnover	8.10	7.89	8.98	10.14	11.63
Accts Payable Turnover	7.24	7.24	7.24	7.24	7.24
Total Asset Turnover	3.66	3.45	2.64	2.11	1.82

Debt Ratios	FY2004	FY2005	FY2006	FY2007	FY2008
Debt to Net Worth	0.90	0.73	0.43	0.27	0.19
Short-Term Liab. to Liab.	1.00	1.00	1.00	1.00	1.00

Liquidity Ratios	FY2004	FY2005	FY2006	FY2007	FY2008
Current Ratio	1.75	2.24	3.29	4.71	6.19
Quick Ratio	1.02	1.64	2.76	4.23	5.72
Net Working Capital	$110,265	$399,068	$1,312,976	$3,528,643	$8,814,324
Interest Coverage	22.72	39.42	73.26	124.67	229.16

Additional Ratios	FY2004	FY2005	FY2006	FY2007	FY2008
Assets to Sales	0.27	0.29	0.38	0.47	0.55
Debt/Assets	47%	42%	30%	21%	16%
Current Debt/Total Assets	47%	42%	30%	21%	16%
Acid Test	0.82	1.43	2.53	3.96	5.42
Asset Turnover	3.66	3.45	2.64	2.11	1.82
Sales/Net Worth	6.97	5.97	3.78	2.67	2.17
Dividend Payout	$0	$0	$0	$0	$0

8.8 Conclusion

ABC MANUFACTURING is a company that provides superior products and consulting that far exceed what is in the market today. Our executive team is highly capable of achieving the goals and objectives set forth in this business plan. In addition, our products provide much needed relief from challenge. ABC MANUFACTURING is a progressive company and is expanding to new heights. The products are in demand and the new product designs are being well accepted.

With the advent of retail sales and television shopping networks, the sales will increase over previous years. In order to meet the demands that these two divisions are anticipated to generate, investment into the growth of the Company will need to occur.

APPENDIX

- Testimonials

- Month-by-Month Financial Projections

- Marketing Materials (in printed and bound version of the business plan)

Index

NOTES

NOTES